FINDING GOD'S PATH IN A DARK SEASON

PASTOR KEN & ALISON DAVIDSON

Finding God's Path in a Dark Season
Copyright © 2017 by Ken & Alison Davidson

Paperback – ISBN: 978-0-9934910-9-2
Ebook – ISBN: 978-1-9997955-0-4

Published by
Maurice Wylie Media
Bethel Media House
Tobermore
Magherafelt,
Northern Ireland
BT45 5SG (UK)

Publishers' statement: Throughout this book the love for our God is such that whenever we refer to Him we honour with Capitals. On the other hand, when referring to the devil, we refuse to acknowledge him with any honour to the point of violating grammatical rule and withholding capitalisation.

For more information visit
www.MauriceWylieMedia.com

Contents

ENDORSEMENTS

"This is a powerful story! But it is also a lovely story of how God can take a young man bound by sin, steeped in drugs trying to ease the frustrations of life, and make him into a child of God and then make him into a Servant of God.

The words of the Lord Jesus were fulfilled in this young man's life when He said: "Follow me and I will make you to become fishers of men." Little did Ken Davidson know when he surrendered his life to the Lord Jesus what he would become!

It's a great honour and a great pleasure to be associated with this young man for God's hand is upon him. It's also wonderful to see how God has given him a lovely wife and family who stand with him and support him in all that he does for the Kingdom of God. It is many years now since Ken wandered into the Metropolitan Tabernacle Belfast and heard the claims of Christ and responded to those claims, resulting in a changed life.

The title of this book fits him completely, *Finding God's Path In a Dark Season.* Read it my friend and be encouraged but not only encouraged, be inspired, inspired like Ken to attempt great things for God and His Kingdom."

Yours in His service,

Pastor James McConnell,

(Retired Senior Pastor) Whitewell Metropolitan Church, Belfast.

"Ken Davidson is one of the good guys! I have known him, his wife Alison and their children for a number of years and I consider him to be a true friend, a fellow labourer and soldier in the fight of faith. He has a passion for God's truth revealed in Holy Scripture and is not ashamed to declare the whole counsel of God in times of apostasy and lukewarmness. I heartily recommend this book of his life and ministry in various vineyards and know you will be encouraged and inspired at what you read."

Pastor David Purse

Senior Pastor, Whitewell Metropolitan Tabernacle, Belfast.

*****

"We first got to know Ken and Alison during the Saturday night house meetings in Belfast from around 2002. Ken and Jolene did testimony videos around the same time that were produced and distributed across Northern Ireland which helped forge a bond between the families.

We got to know Pastor Ken as a dear friend, attending morning prayer meetings, what was then every Friday morning at 6am before work, over the course of several years. That little group of people in prayer became united in focus and had a heart for God to move in Belfast and Northern Ireland. Over the last 15 years, Ken and Alison have always inspired us, as humble and gracious servants of the Lord. We have seen them as an example and a couple to emulate in our own personal lives and ministries. Through their experience as missionaries, and church leaders, their wisdom and guidance has enriched our lives. We revere their ability to overcome challenging circumstances in ministry, with humility, not giving into bitterness or despair. That for us, has been an inspiration. Ken's bible knowledge is extensive and he always knows how to connect bible prophecy to current world affairs. He teaches with boldness and courage in the face of opposition. His willingness to suffer loss for the sake of the truth is something that is precious and rare in our generation and we thank God for his passion for souls. We have admired Alison's sweet spirit and unassuming kindness, and her intimate relationship with the Master is evident when she opens her mouth to pray. May the Lord richly bless them and continue to pour out His Spirit upon their lives, their family and their ministry."

Pastor Jason and Jolene Allen
Missionaries, Metropolitan Tabernacle Ministries, Nyeri, Kenya.

*****

"I have known Pastor Ken Davidson and His wife Alison for several years now and I have found them to be a family who are totally committed to the work of the Lord and to His people. Pastor Ken Davidson is a very capable Bible teacher and that has come from many years of devoted study. They have been through many difficult times and trials and they have taken this and demonstrated the provision and protection of their Lord and Saviour, Jesus Christ.

I would thoroughly recommend *'Finding God's Path In a Dark Season'* to everyone and especially to the unsaved that they may see God's goodness in the lives of this faithful couple."

Dr Alan Stephens
Senior Pastor, Church of God, Glenmachan, Belfast.

*****

"I remember Pastor Ken Davidson when I was a young lad growing up in Whitewell Church. I always remembered Ken having a passion for the lost and preaching in the open air. This is where I saw a man who desired people to come to know Christ. Pastor Ken's ministry over the years has went from strength to strength due to his love and faithfulness to the lord. His ministry is dynamic and fruitful and many people have been inspired, encouraged and saved by the preaching by this servant of God. His story will be inspirational and heart touching and will encourage you to draw closer to our glorious Saviour."

Lee McClelland

Leader of Teen Challenge, Belfast and Pastor of The Ark Church, Belfast.

*****

"I have known Pastor Ken Davidson some 20 years now. I have found him to be one of the great preachers of today. His gift for expounding the Word of God is captivating. Naturally, Pastor Ken entered this world the same as all of you. Ken wasn't always a pastor and experienced quite a lot of the troubles in Northern Ireland. The title of his book *'Finding God's Path in a Dark Season,'* reveals much in regards to the road he came down and his experience with drink and drugs. Truly a wild character before he met Jesus Christ as his Saviour. Only Jesus could calm the storm in this man's life. If there is one person I would call a 'Trophy Of Grace' through Jesus Christ, it is Pastor Ken Davidson. Now he is one of those people you love to be with. I couldn't recommend this book to you highly enough. A must read!"

Pastor Laurence Edgar (Senior)

Tabernacle Pentecostal Church, Belfast.

*****

"The first time I met Ken and Alison Davidson in 2010, I immediately realised that I had met an exceptional couple. Since then, in our years of friendship, they have proven themselves to be people of sterling character, and able ministers of the Gospel of Jesus Christ. Pastor Davidson has been a real blessing in his ministry of the Word of God and an encouragement to many, not only in his home country but also in the United States. It has been our privilege to enjoy the warm fellowship of Ken and Alison and to be blessed by their rich ministry. They have shown sincere love for the Lord's people in their service to Christ and have remained faithful to their convictions during times of hardship and opposition. Ken and Alison are truly genuine and faithful friends and an invaluable God-given gift to the body of Christ."

Pastor Charles & Marylee Jennings,

Truth In History Ministry, Oklahoma, USA.

*****

"I have known my good friends, Pastor Ken Davidson, Alison and family for many years now, having grown up with them at the Metropolitan Tabernacle, Belfast. I have witnessed first-hand their remarkable journey of faith, from the first day until now, they are both trophies of God's amazing grace and great testimonies of God's great saving and keeping power. As a chosen vessel of the Lord, Pastor Ken as a servant of Christ has without doubt been raised up, being equipped with not only the heart of David to shepherd the flock. But also with the power and prophetic ministry of Elijah, to stand as a watchman on Zion's walls, trumpeting the Gospel message to a wayward nation, exhorting its people to turn back to God. Personally, Pastor Ken has been a Bible Barnabas; a man with a kingdom mentality, one of integrity and a true companion in the Gospel. Of Pastor Ken's ministry over the years he is not an 'either or' preacher.... He's a 'both and' preacher, a man of not only the word but of the Spirit. One of a very few in the nation called with the task of repairing this breach. Isaiah 58:12. Prepare to be blessed, encouraged and challenged as you open the pages of this book. God bless!"

Stuart Elliott

Evangelist and founder of One Goal Ministries, International Footballer for Northern Ireland (2000-2007)

DEDICATION

We dedicate this book to both our families, to those who are gone but never forgotten and to those who are still here with us. We especially dedicate it to our two beautiful and amazing daughters, Jodie and Ellie who have grown up being Pastor's kids; with the stresses and trials it brings even to their own lives and the expectations made of them. We love you both.

We also would dedicate this to our shepherd and mentor in the faith, Pastor James McConnell who has been instrumental through God's grace in making ministry possible for us, but more so, in showing us Christ in all the Scriptures and teaching us through the Holy Spirit to love the Lord Jesus Christ.

INTRODUCTION

KEN...

Whether we are a good Christian, a lukewarm Christian or a non-Christian, at some point in our life a 'dark season' will close in on us. The good news is... it can be in those darkest seasons that we sense God the most. It is then, I have felt God the closest and have gained the most experience. It is from that place that I want to help others.

Many times I've asked the Lord; "Why me? Why save me? Why bless me? Why love me?" I guess it's something I'll never comprehend. I could say like the Apostle Paul in 1 Timothy 1:15 *'That Christ Jesus came into the world to save sinners of whom I am chief.'* The impossibility of my finding out the full depths of the sovereign grace and immeasurable love of God towards me is equal to my inability to save myself. I rejoice in divine mercy that *'while I was yet a sinner, Christ died for me.'* (Romans 5:8) There's no darker season nor place to be than without Christ as He is God's path in the dark season of every life.

This book is written to help those who are in a hopeless condition as they travel through dark valleys to remind them that *'to every thing there is a season and a time to every purpose under the heaven.'* (Ecclesiastes 3:1) In this book you will see dark seasons both before and after our conversion to Christ but we learned not to dwell there but to see His glory in every situation of our life and how great His love is for us and that same love reaches out to you. Scripture states in Psalms 32:8; *'I will instruct thee and teach thee in the way which thou shalt go: I will guide thee with mine eye.'*

There are different valleys that everyone encounters in their lives. We may not go through them all but one valley that we will all experience is the valley of tears. That valley can be the loss of a loved one, a dream that came to a sudden end, removal of a car or a house, or the doctor saying; "I can do nothing more for you!"

Always remember, when a dark season closes it, the sun still shines behind those dark clouds. Likewise, the Son, Jesus Christ our Lord still reigns no matter what stands in front of us! Did He, Jesus not say, *"I will never leave thee, nor forsake thee?"* Hebrews 13:5.

Puritan, Samuel Rutherford once said; "Since He looked upon me, my heart is not my own, He hath run away to heaven with it." The Lord Jesus Christ now owns our heart. Both Alison and my own as one in Him and when He is your heart's desire then He is your treasure from above. Dark seasons may blur the path from view but Christ's own are never out of His sight. We trust you will receive encouragement to keep going on with God and receive a blessing knowing that He is. THIS SAME JESUS.

ALISON...

Throughout our Christian walk, we all encounter mountains and valleys. We have walked through our fair share of valleys and God has brought us through every time. We have come through great seasons of loss and times where it has felt that all hope was gone.

Sometimes God leads you down unexpected paths and some paths may have steep inclines or sharp, unexpected twists and turns but no matter where or how the path leads you, it's learning to trust the Shepherd who is just ahead, making the path straight, clearing the path of any unseen dangers and lighting the path with His lamp.

As it says in Psalm 119:105; *'Thy word is a lamp unto my feet, and a light unto my path.'*

So, we hope that by sharing some of our experiences and by showing you how God has lead us on different paths, this book will be like a lamp that will shine into your circumstances and light up the way more clearly for you on your journey.

I know from personal experience, it is very easy to look back and say; "Oh look at the lessons we learned through that, look what God did there." However, it's when you are in the midst of the storm, the path that you once saw so clearly in front, can then be tainted, so badly that you no longer see where you are going.

During our time in Donaghcloney, I believe God gave me Scripture for Ken for the kind of preacher and pastor that our land requires, it's found in Isaiah 58:8-12;

'Then shall thy light break forth as the morning, and thine health shall spring forth speedily: and thy righteousness shall go before thee; the glory of the Lord shall be thy reward. Then shalt thou call, and the Lord shall answer; thou shalt cry, and he shall say, Here I am. If thou take away from the midst of thee the yoke, the putting forth

of the finger, and speaking vanity; And if thou draw out thy soul to the hungry, and satisfy the afflicted soul; then shall thy light rise in obscurity, and thy darkness be as the noonday: and the Lord shall guide thee continually, and satisfy thy soul in drought, and make fat thy bones: and thou shalt be like a watered garden, and like a spring of water, whose waters fail not. And they that shall be of thee shall build the old waste places: thou shalt raise up the foundations of many generations; and thou shalt be called, The repairer of the breach, The restorer of paths to dwell in.'

Ken would rebuild the old waste places and be a restorer of the paths to dwell in. Ken was to be an old-time Pentecostal preacher never removing or changing God's word but rather holding to God's truth, (John 17:17) standing up for biblical principles no matter the cost. *'Remove not the ancient landmark, which thy fathers have set.'* Proverbs 22:28.

We pray that by reading this book you will see how God has lead and taught us to repair the breeches and restore the old paths, so that others can walk the path with less stumbling and walk more in God's marvellous light. Allow me to share my failings, but also my victories as a mum and a wife to my God-given husband, Ken.

Section 1

The Paths of God's Direction

'Shew me thy ways, O Lord; teach me thy paths.'

Psalm 25:4

Chapter One
Keeping on the straight and narrow...

Walking through life it is inevitable that many will stray from the path that God has laid out for them. According to Scripture, this path is set even before we took our first breath in the world. The book of Jeremiah 1:5 states; *'Before I formed thee in the belly I knew thee; and before thou camest forth out of the womb I sanctified thee, and I ordained thee a prophet unto the nations.'*

Did you read that? The God of the universe knew all about me before I was even formed. He knows us and He loves us, despite our past and future actions. Does that not blow your mind? It blows my mind!

I know when I look back over my life I have made a lot of mistakes, some of which I will share in this book. The good news is, no matter how dark a season we enter, remember this, the God of all creation knows you, He formed you, because He has a plan for you!

Even though at times, I certainly have failed the Lord, His love for me and you never changes. He loves you and I unconditionally, He's a good Father! As the Scripture promises; *'For I am persuaded, that neither death, nor life, nor angels, nor principalities, nor powers, nor things present, nor things to come, nor height, nor depth, nor any other creature, shall be able to separate us from the love of God, which is in Christ Jesus our Lord.'* Romans 8:38-39.

Ken's Story

Before I came to know the Lord, I had quite a troubled and humble beginning.

I was born in 1966 in the Templemore Avenue hospital in East Belfast, Northern Ireland. We lived in a small house off the Albertbridge Road called Mourne Street.

'The Troubles'[1] broke out in 1969 and East Belfast was very volatile. Paramilitaries from both communities roamed everywhere as they sought to dominate with fear and intimidation, with shootings and bombs. Obviously, as I was still very young at that time I don't remember a lot of things, but even though my mind did not understand a lot of *why* things were happening, fear was still gripping me as I was waking up in cold sweats, absolutely shaking. Several times my parents took me to the doctor about this and the doctor said that I was obviously picking up on all the violence going on around me. It was having a deep psychological impact on me so the decision was made to move out of that area. I was only five, when our family moved to the Shore Road in North Belfast. My granny and grandad Davidson and other members of our family lived in North Belfast so it made sense to move there.

One of my first memories of moving to the Shore Road was seeing my first 'parade.' Now for many of you who are reading this book, especially those of you from outside Northern Ireland. I may just need to explain what I mean by a 'parade.' The street that our house was on, was closed off with barricades, made from large barrels, cement blocks and basically anything the paramilitaries could find. Walking down the middle of the road was an army of men marching in sync. With the narrow streets of Belfast their steps

---

1   'The Troubles' refer to the years 1969–1997 in Northern Ireland where over 3,500 were murdered by gun or bomb. The conflict was between nationalists (mainly self-identified as Roman Catholic) and unionists (mainly self-identified as Protestant).

echoed louder as their boots hit the road. Wearing camouflaged combat jackets and green berets, most of the men wore some form of mask. This had quite an impact on me, as other children may have had swings or slides to play on, in many areas in Northern Ireland, like mine, the children's playground was a war zone with nearby houses having been bombed or residents driven out by the opposing side. We learned to play hide and seek in those derelict buildings... life for a child... well what can I say?

My mum, Violet was a home-help. This was someone who the government employed to visit people who qualified for help around their own homes. She would have visited people early in the morning, cleaning the house, washing dishes etc. She also worked in a wholesale pharmacy. My dad was a vehicle mechanic but not just an ordinary one, I'll go into this more later. Elaine was my eldest sister, I had a younger sister called Heather and a younger brother called Stephen.

Our 'wee' (small) house had no heating with only two bedrooms for the six of us. For a while the four of us shared a big bed and then through time my dad converted the attic so my sisters could move up there. The house was very basic, it didn't even have a bathroom. Instead, we had an outdoor toilet and had to use public baths to get washed. We had a very small yard but my dad was able to build an outhouse, it had just a corrugated plastic roof but it gave us a kitchen as the house didn't have one. There was no hot water, we just had a geyser with a small hot flame. The house was really damp, in fact, it was so damp that my dad wallpapered the kitchen walls with tin foil! Yes, seriously! He did this to try and prevent the water running down it. Even the frogs I gathered from the river, were able to live out at the back of the house, they loved the dampness, but I'm not sure my mum loved them!

When our next-door neighbour died, their house became derelict, the neighbours that moved in did not have two legs but four as it became a haven for mice and one house was not big enough for them, it wasn't long before they had come across into our house. Without doubt, it was dire living conditions.

I remember my younger sister Heather was so ashamed of our home that when she was dating her boyfriend, that she would tell him that the toilet was broken so he would never realise that we didn't actually have one inside the house.

Even though my parents had purchased their own house in the 70's from the Housing Executive, (the Northern Ireland Housing body) we ended up actually worse off. A number of months later when the Housing Executive was upgrading all their houses on the street to receive indoor bathrooms. Guess who didn't get one? Us! We didn't qualify.

For us to have a bath, we had to go up to the *Grove Baths* to wash ourselves. Those thirty minutes sessions in *Grove Baths* that one was allowed each time was our normality.

My parents...

My mum was a real loving mother, very maternal. She was the sort that could have done without so her children would have. As we would say in Northern Ireland, she was 'the height of nothing,' she was only five-foot tall. (152cms) She was small but was a wee dynamo, she was always on the go. But as small as she was and as soft as she was, if there was ever anyone giving off to, or threatening her children, she turned into a lioness.

One of her greatest qualities was giving.

The Bible states, '*Give, and it shall be given unto you; good measure, pressed down, and shaken together, and running over, shall men give into your bosom. For with the same measure that ye mete withal it shall be measured to you again.*' Luke 6:38.

Luke 6:38 is notorious for being used throughout the church for giving to people that we know, especially the preacher! But did you know this portion refers to giving to the unknown person, the neighbour or even your enemy? Let's read a few verses earlier…

'For if ye love them which love you, what thank have ye? for sinners also love those that love them. And if ye do good to them which do good to you, what thank have ye? for sinners also do even the same. And if ye lend to them of whom ye hope to receive, what thank have ye? for sinners also lend to sinners, to receive as much again. Luke 6:32-35.

Did you read that Scripture? Sinners (ungodly) love their own but we as the Church need to reach out past our own and it was my mum who set that example to me while I was young. She was a giver, never fearful to give or to step over the line of ordinary giving, i.e. just looking after her own. I witnessed it many times, it was just her nature to give. For example, in the 70's there was a family moved in across the street and they didn't have an easy time of it from the local community, because they were Indian Sikhs. In those day's there were not many Sikh families in Northern Ireland. One day I came home from school and my mum had all five children sitting on our settee. Their mother had been delayed from work and instead of allowing the children to stand out on the street, my mum brought them in and fed them with what little we had. She saw a need, and in seeing the need, she stepped out!

Let me challenge us here by saying, is there a need that you know about that you can reach into and be Christ's hand to someone?

You will never know how far a seed of love, compassion and help can go! After all, Scripture states, *'But God commendeth (made a stand with) his love toward us, while we were yet sinners, Christ died for us.'* Romans 5:8.

Read this carefully, while I, Ken Davidson was sinning, or going to sin, God in His love reached across a boundary of such a great divide and caught me at my worst and led me into His sheepfold. We too can reach across that which divides or separates us from those around us and be onto the Christ who dwells within us.

When it came to disciplining us, my mum would have said; "I am going to smack you." She used to lightly tap me and I would have mockingly said; "Aww that's terrible." Her love for me sought to correct me but not to hurt me!

My friend, God is love and in that, every correction comes from love and based on that love, He corrects and instructs us showing a way out.

'And ye have forgotten the exhortation which speaketh unto you as unto children, My son, despise not thou the chastening of the Lord, nor faint when thou art rebuked of him.' Hebrews 12:5. However, like us all, we have another side, which we don't advertise. I think my mum would have made a good gunslinger! She always wore a wee pair of slippers on her feet around the house and within seconds of us kids misbehaving, she could have taken one of those slippers off and it would have been coming through the air at you. Before you would have seen it, BANG! It always hit us at the right spot!

My Dad...

My dad always loved working at cars but after a few years working in several different garages as a mechanic, he applied for a job which if he got, would change our lives. The day came when he received the letter, he had been accepted as a mechanic for the UDR.[2] My dad was always a hard worker and desired for our lives to be better like any true father wants. Although getting the job in the UDR made him a high-risk target to the IRA terrorists, for him it was providing food on the table for those whom he loved.

When I look back, I can see the hours that my dad spent working sometimes even through the night to keep the Land Rover jeeps for the UDR moving, his commitment was for the security of our country and the welfare of our family.

Because of my father's work ethic, he was promoted to head

2   The Ulster Defence Regiment was the largest infantry regiment of the British Army. Established in 1970 - 1992. During 'The Troubles' 258 UDR personnel were murdered, most of which were murdered off-duty.

mechanic. Overseeing now a team of mechanics and keeping the UDR battalion on the go. With that came the danger and quite often he would have been called out to recover a broken-down Land Rover in the midst of a gun-battle. With bullets bouncing all around him, my dad would be lying under the Land Rover with his toolkit trying to get it going!

The IRA received most of their information on potential targets from their sympathisers. These IRA sympathisers would pass on information to the IRA about who was in the UDR and then in turn, my dad became a target. He was in danger, we therefore as a family were all in danger.

I remember how our house phone rang, once the call ended, my dad would rush us all into the back of the house, which would have been more secure from a street gun attack on our home. The call would have been from the local barracks saying that an attack was possible. As we entered the small room at the back, he would have barred the doors and locked the house down. This happened when an IRA informer would have tipped off the police about who was in danger on a list of death threats.

We would have sat huddled as a family waiting either for an attack or a call from the Ministry Of Defence to say it was clear. Other times when things were more serious we would have been held up in that room until the army or police came and sealed off the area. Many times, as a young boy going to bed at night even though I was being raised in a non-Christian home, I would try and pray while in my bed. With fear on my face I would pray; "Please God don't let these men get my dad, please don't let them come into this house, please don't let them take my dad." I remember being very afraid at night, not just one night but every single night.

When possible, dad would have taken us camping to the lovely lakes of Enniskillen or up to the famous views of the North Coast to try and get away from all the tension and fear.

Scripture states about being weak as in Joel 3:10, '...*let the weak say, I am strong.*'

We all have a weakness and my dad's weakness was old bangers! They were his favourite type of car to drive. One time, he got a lovely blue Vauxhall Victor and we thought we were like famous Hollywood actors in a limousine. We just thought it was the best ever! It was a big car and he loved it.

One Summer we all went camping and had a wonderful time. Arriving back in Belfast, we were so hungry that we left the car packed with the camping gear, sleeping bags and a tank of gas for the camp stove, and went inside, After eating our supper we would then go out and unpack the car. Dad finished first and when he went outside we heard him shouting; "Where is my car?"

Previous to this, he had already three cars stolen from just outside our front door and while trying to remain calm, he reported his most recent car to the police, as stolen.

His precious Victor was a goner! A few hours passed by and the phone rang, the army had found the car. We hurried round to the location where major disappointment was soon on all of our faces. The army had blown the car up, it was in pieces! Due to the security threat in Northern Ireland, when the car was discovered by the police, the army had to send in the bomb disposal unit as they saw a tank of gas hidden under the camping gear – they thought it was a home-made bomb! They thought the IRA had planted it, so poor Victor got blown to bits, the army not realising it was just our camping equipment.

Like most children in Northern Ireland who had a parent in the security forces, our home-life was not normal. We would never be allowed to stand near the windows at home, especially at night, dad would have shouted; "Get away from that window!" Obviously in case the house would have been shot at. Every time we were to travel in the car, even if we left the car in the town and came back to it after shopping, my dad would have searched underneath it for explosives and booby-traps. At school, we weren't allowed to talk about our dad to anybody. If the chat arose regarding a question about my dad's job, I was told to say he was a mechanic. I wasn't allowed to say where he worked, where he went to, who he knew - just that he was a car mechanic. During those years the IRA tried to murder my dad several times.

Early one Sunday morning in Belfast while most people were still in bed, my dad was going to work in his car. Driving along, he saw a man that looked to have been injured lying on the side of the road, another man was standing waving dad down signalling for help. My dad was slowing down to stop and see if he could help when all of a sudden, the two terrorists pulled out guns to shoot at him. My dad was able to speed off and made it safely to the barracks. The very next week on the same road, a JCB pulled out in front of my dad's mate who was in the UDR. The terrorists kidnapped him and he was later found tortured to death. As a family, we never spoke much about it, but in the back of all of our minds, we thought, that could have been my dad. Again, his life had been spared.

One day while he was at work his mate asked to change shifts with him at the weekend, my dad, obliging as he always was, swapped with him. On that weekend shift, instead of my dad being where he normally would be, his mate was there. Terrorists opened fire from a derelict building overlooking the army camp and sprayed him with automatic fire. My dad's mate was shot in the stomach and face but he survived. That shook my dad to his core as he knew that it could have been him. Again, his life had been spared but it was a close-call.

My dad's weakness was his passion and even Godly men had passions. In James 5:17; *'Elias* (Elijah) *was a man subject to like passions as we are.'* Sometimes when a passion consumes, common-sense goes out of the window. In-fact with all of this danger around my dad, I wondered what he was thinking. I remember arriving home from school in the 80's, I had noticed a very bright yellow Volkswagen Golf sitting outside our front door. I thought we had visitors. It wasn't long before I found out, we had no visitors, it was not the neighbours' car, it was my dad's! It was like a colour from another universe, it even glowed in the dark! I am not joking!

Here we were trying to stay under the radar from terrorists. Trying to make it as difficult for them not to see us coming and here comes, 'glow in the dark' really shouting; "Hey terrorists I am over here!" If you have a passion, make sure you have balance with it!

Alison's Story

In comparison to Ken, I had a very privileged upbringing. Anything I wanted, my parents got it for me. The area I was raised in saw very little of 'The Troubles' when I was a child. My Dad, Stan worked as a prison officer in the Maze and my mum worked as a care assistant. I had one older brother called Jed. I was like the female version of the prodigal son (Luke 15:11-32) in the Bible. I did not lack for anything and yet, everything that was being handed to me, was not enough. Like the prodigal son, I started to rebel. I thought, I don't want this, this isn't the type of home I want to be in. When I think of it now, if this was one of our two daughters, I would have had a heavy heart.

At the age of fourteen I was totally off the rails. The prodigal joined himself to a citizen of that country, I joined every rave club I could come across. A popular place for rebellious teenagers was a club in Banbridge. It was meant to be a rave club but really it was just a drug den. Back then rave music had really just come out and was very popular but it was heavily associated with drugs. My first memory of walking into this place, was like walking into a sweetie shop but instead of sweets, it was full of drugs. I was in my element, a cosy home with parents who lifted and laid me, money when required and an adventure in the darkness that seemed to be becoming more regular than not. Life for me, was going from party to party with my friends.

Things were good, however, at the age of fifteen my body started to feel weak, I would faint without warning and my parents were worried. When my symptoms continued, they eventually took me to see a consultant. My life was about to change, I was diagnosed with M.E. and for the next six months I was bed-ridden. My mum literally had to do everything for me. Even at that young age I learned a valuable lesson. Those who walk with you in the light of your day can be many. But when the night comes, and at some point, it does come. Friends becomes few if any. For me it was when I couldn't go out the door, when I couldn't buy them the drinks any more, when four walls became my whole life for a year. It is then that one gets to know who your true friends are.

My M.E. battle...

Whenever I took ill, the doctors had no idea what it was. They were so baffled they were actually testing me for leukaemia. Then there was the conflict of, was I just putting this on? Some days I would have woken up feeling not too bad but by the time I would have got to school, I was exhausted.

I was at Dromore High School at the time and we had some mobile units in the grounds, walking from the mobile to the main school building would have wiped me out and it was such a short distance, it made no sense. I remember after walking into school, the sweat would have been pouring off me and I was really breathless. I looked and felt like I had ran a marathon, my body was aching and my mind was foggy. On a continual basis I was being sent home as I just needed to be in bed. I remember this continued for a long time until it came to a peak. One day my body just shut down.

At that time I was starting to take panic attacks and I remember this was a particularly bad one, I thought I was going to die. The school called my mum and I was taken to a different doctor that day. As I had taken this massive panic attack, I was able to see a doctor who specialises in breathing and whenever he sat down and we went through my symptoms, he recognised straight away what it was, because his wife had M.E. This was the breakthrough my family needed as he was able to officially diagnose me with the condition. He gave me a book and told me to go home and read it.

Finally, everything started making sense, all the information in the book was what I was experiencing. The symptoms matched completely my feelings, I felt relieved that at last someone was understanding what was happening to me. It let me see that it wasn't in my head, I wasn't going nuts, I wasn't depressed, I wasn't dying but I was ill.

By that stage I really was bed-bound and mum had to shower me and feed me. Just everything you would hate as a teenager, you can imagine how undignified it felt for me. During those months, I was only lifted in and out of bed by my parents for getting washed. It was just awful, the illness consumed my whole body. I was suffering with tiredness, had sore muscles like I had ran a marathon. I had severe tension headaches, migraine headaches, poor appetite, weight loss, terrible pale skin and an awful sleep pattern. I woke up tired, I felt isolated, had black eyes, was dizzy with vomiting and suffered frequent panic attacks. The panic attacks were the worst. I started to shut down, they were very frequent. One night I took a really bad attack and my mum rang the doctor, he suggested getting a brown paper bag for me to breath in and out of to regulate my breathing. From that night on, brown paper bags went with me everywhere I went. The panic attacks were really scary, I really feared that I was dying. I could feel my heart pounding right out of my chest. Because of my heart racing, my whole body was affected. I could feel pins and needles in my hands, my legs, even my nose and around my mouth. I was really afraid to be on my own as I really feared death. Sometimes the panic attacks came on me while I was sleeping, I would have woken up in a sweat, my body shaking then I was sick afterwards. My mum was terrified too and she had no help as every time she rang the doctor she was just advised to use the paper bag. It must have been awful for her. At that time, there was very little awareness of M.E. even among the doctors. Most of our family didn't understand what was wrong. She didn't get much support from people herself as they thought it was all in my head, I remember people saying to her; "M.E. that's what it is – it's all about ME!"

I was offered anti-depressants to try and settle me but I wasn't depressed, I was ill. I was sent to a specialist in Belfast City Hospital and I can remember the ordeal of trying to get there, it was such a nightmare trying to do it without me passing out, as the journey was going to use up all my strength. We had to take a basin with us as I was feeling really sick, I was really worried about going to a busy hospital. My parents just made me a bed in the back seat of the car and I tried to lie there for the long journey. I was concerned I was going to take a panic attack but at the same time I was hopeful that this specialist could cure me. To be honest, it was a real let-down. He gave me a chart, it was just like a calendar where I was to write down whether I was having a good day or a bad day and every day at that time was a bad day! For me a good day would be that I could get up to the living room to sit for an hour before going back to bed. The only other thing he gave me was multi-vitamin tablets, they were huge, really hard to swallow. He just advised to start taking small steps and building myself up. I was so frustrated, he had absolutely nothing to offer me. As there was no cure, he told me to just rest and work with it.

I was so restricted by my body and what I could and couldn't do within the limits of it. I was just unable to do hardly anything for quite a long period of time. This was such a huge change for me as growing up I was always on the go. I was out every night socialising with friends at some event or other. I just loved to be busy as it took my mind off other things.

Looking at it now, I do see God's hand was with me then, as I know where I would have gone if I hadn't of been ill. The girl I was best friends with at the time just went nuts, she dated a drug dealer and ran away from home and I would have been daft enough to have went along with her. I believe the Lord used my illness to set me aside and just said; "No."

Although, if I had only thought about that at the time, I might have learned my lesson but no, as soon as I did gather my strength I was wanting to make up for my lost time.

It took me a long time to get myself back together, it was about a year and a half before I was really feeling more normal again. During that time I missed my GCSE exams as I couldn't concentrate. I was given a tutor who visited me at home for a couple of hours but she could have been teaching me anything, I just couldn't take it in.

Through time I started to gradually build my body up, with the help of doctors we devised a plan. First step was walking from the front door to the gate and back into the house. This was all I was allowed to do, I did this every day and then gradually I was walking out around the house. Then the next step was adjusting my time clock, we had to work to getting me awake during the day and sleeping at night. It had been advised to jump-start my body that I should take a really cold shower. Those cold showers were awful. We tried everything, my poor dad devoted himself to researching every possible herbal remedy that was available. It felt like my day was filled with taking tablets and drops. They made me drink Guinness and cooked me liver as I was very low in iron. Some of the things helped but there was no magical cure.

On the road to recovery...

When I did recover I went to Banbridge Technical College to do Health and Social Care studies. To be honest, I tried to get some sort of education but partying and having a good time was much more important to me. I wanted to have a life rather than a certificate!

At the age of seventeen I was going off on binge holidays and doing all the crazy things I could think of doing. Going out on a Saturday night was what I lived for, that was the height of excitement. I loved getting all dressed up.

After I finished my course, I couldn't decide what I wanted to have a career in, so I thought about doing nursing. An opportunity came up for me and my friend to go to Scotland, we had heard about an aptitude test that you did and if you passed you get instantly into nursing. I thought this was a great idea, and a shortcut to nursing! Instead of having to do all this education, here was a quick way into nursing. We studied hard for the aptitude test and went to Scotland. When the results were given, I failed by one mark and my friend failed by two. We decided to study a bit more so we could take the test again and pass it, but they told us that they were really desperate for nurses and as we had only missed the pass mark slightly, to come on ahead and they would get us work as nurses, they were sure we would get the test next time. So we packed up our things and were brought over to Scotland by my mum and dad on the ferry. They dropped us off at our student digs in Paisley, just outside Glasgow. We had our car packed with our best shoes and clothes but not a winter woolly in sight! I couldn't wait to start my new life in Scotland. This was going to be my fresh start, free from everyone and everything. A new career ahead in nursing, it was going to be brilliant.

My friend and I thought that we could catch up with our old school friends who had moved over to Scotland too. Most of them went to Glasgow University, we met up and they were showing us the sights of Glasgow and before we knew it, we were out clubbing. We were out all night, absolutely pie-eyed and not one of us had the aptitude to set an alarm for the test the next morning. So, we completely missed the entire test - the whole reason for going in the first place! The next test wasn't for another six months so here we were in Scotland, stuck with nothing to do until then. We didn't know what to do so we signed on the dole. We then continued to live in this little house that we fondly named 'the Igloo' as it was so cold.

The stubbornness rose in me, instead of calling my mum and just telling her that I had messed up and asking her to bring me home, I was determined to make it work. I wasn't going to go home to listen to 'I told you so...' Or 'Far off fields are green...' I decided that I was staying in Scotland no matter what. I told my room-mate that we needed to get jobs, we had to make life work there. When I think back now, we must have been stinking! In the six weeks we were there, we washed our clothes once. The house was so cold you couldn't function normally, we just kept adding more layers to keep us warm. We actually stayed in bed one day, all day as we were so cold.

It was around this time that the Lord started working in my life. I remember in Scotland just feeling so dissatisfied with everything going on, I really felt like life just wasn't measuring up for me. The cold in the house was getting worse so we decided to get a Superser gas heater but of course we had no money for the tank of gas. I rang my mum and asked her to send me over some money, she put £25 into my bank account. Well, I thought I was rich! My friend and I talked about the money, we wondered if we should use it to buy gas and some food or maybe we should go mad and have a fun day out in Glasgow? So needless to say, we went out for the night in Glasgow and had a blast. It was a great idea at the time but the next day, things seemed even more bleak than before. We were back to being penniless, freezing and hungry.

My friend had enough that day, she decided to phone her mummy and told her she was going home. This left me with no choice but to go home. Arriving back, I went through a depression, nothing satisfied me and I really was unhappy with everything. I got employment in the local nursing home and fell back into my routine of life, working all week for the purpose of going out on Saturday night. When Mum and Dad went off on their holidays that was always an excuse for me to have a party. One time while they were away, I had a full coach of people come round to my parents' house. By the time the coach arrived from an Enniskillen nightclub, most of the people on it, were drunk. During the night someone had decided to leave their cider cans in mums closet and worse still, someone broke the window in my brother Jed's pigeon sheds. Of course, I didn't realise, but all the pigeons escaped and they were prize-winning birds, worth a lot of money.

So, when my parents arrived home, and the party evidence was found, I was in the 'doghouse' for a long time after that, but it never dampened my desire to either be in a party or throw a party.

My funeral clothes...

Shortly after I had returned home, my parents were going away for a break so I thought... 'Brilliant, I'll have a party!' I said to my friend about it and we were excited as we thought it would pick us up after the whole Scotland fiasco. The word was passed out that the party was going to be at my parents' house that Saturday night but, instead of the house being filled with people as was usually the case - not one person turned up! We couldn't understand it, not one person arrived.

My friend and I ended up sitting up all night talking about God as we were both brought up in Christian homes. In the middle of our chat we talked about the Lord coming back and an awareness hit the both of us, if Jesus came back tonight, we would not be ready. Would you believe, because of this, the two of us sat in our house reading Bibles! For me, this was so bizarre, so far removed from anything I had done in my life before. That night was the turning part of my life and from that night I really felt the Lord started to strive with me.

Look for the signposts...

When God is in something, He will always leave signposts to help us find our way back to Him. The greatest signpost ever placed in this world was the Cross of Christ and those words that He would say to His disciples... 'Follow Me!' Now, if that is not a signpost I do not know what is. God's GPS (Global Positioning System) is Jesus Christ. When we follow Jesus, peace reigns in our heart and at that point in my life, my heart did not have peace. But God was starting to set up signposts. The question was, was I prepared to follow them? From this time of reading the Bible I started to notice that God had set a signpost up for me in a particular place... the nursing home where I was working. Each day when I was at work, no matter how hard I tried to avoid her, this godly lady would always have met me somewhere and I don't know how she did it. But no matter what she started to talk about, the conversation always went into God. She would keep telling me that the Lord was coming back soon, that she was waiting on Him coming back before she died.

As if I hadn't enough to worry about, I kept thinking to myself... 'Flip, well you are well over 90, if He is coming back before you die, this could be tomorrow.'

Fear has a way of taking good news that 'The Lord is coming back soon,' and making it into news to dread. A couple of nights later, I went to a local hotel and drunk myself sober, I was trying to get away from this fear that the Lord was coming and I was going to miss it. I was running from the signposts God was showing me!

That night I remember walking into our house, all was quiet, mum wasn't waiting for me but she was always worried when I was out, she wouldn't have slept until she was sure I was home safe. I came in and went to bed. Later that night, I noticed that the house seemed quieter than normal. I started to think... 'What if the Lord has come back and I have been left behind? The fear started to rise in me that my mum and dad has been taken, I panicked that I was left behind and that idea of reality started to play on my mind. If that was the case, they had gone to Heaven as they had accepted Jesus Christ as Lord and because I hadn't, then I was not going. Frightful or what?

Shortly after this, I was asked to go to a gospel mission with a friend. Even though it was on a Friday, I agreed to go and told my mum. I will never forget her face, her mouth fell open and I think she nearly passed out! She was shocked enough that I was going to church, let alone it being on a party night! She stood gazing at me for a few seconds then she said; "Alison, you don't have anything appropriate to wear to church." And true enough, neither I did. I only had my clubbing clothes which certainly wouldn't be deemed appropriate by any means. My skirts were all really short, I had no church clothes to wear.

My mum reappeared with what we called, my funeral outfit. It was a horrible long black skirt and a matching top which was on hand for a death in the family. Nothing for it, off I went to church dressed in my funeral clothes.

That night, Pastor Ivan Thompson was preaching and he was so jovial and witty, I really enjoyed listening to him as he spoke on the prodigal son and about him going into the far country. Could this be another signpost? Could God be speaking to me? I thought of my trip to Scotland that I have shared with you and trying to run away from the Lord. I had spent my inheritance and came back with nothing. As my natural parents opened the door again for me, my Spiritual Father in Heaven was showing that He had the door open for me! I could just see the Father running to meet me as portrayed in the book of Luke. I felt a strong call to the Lord as we sang the last hymn to close the meeting...

"Come home! Come home!
Ye who are weary, come home!
Earnestly, tenderly, Jesus is calling,
Calling, O sinner, come home!"

Will L Thompson, 1880.

That night more than ever, I realised I was a sinner in need of a Saviour. Pastor Ivan was shaking everyone's hands as they were leaving the service. I panicked and wondered how we would get out without him speaking to us, so we ran into the toilets. We waited until the people had cleared. When it looked like it was good to go, we bolted for the door.

However, Ivan was on the other side of the door when we went through and he spotted us and began to talk to us. As he brought us back into the church, even though we were reluctantly chatting at the beginning, he and his wife led us to the Lord that night. I was nineteen at the time and that was the start of my walk with God.

Chapter Two
Getting caught...

As a young boy, I really looked up to my father. He was a loving dad but he was a disciplinarian, very unlike my mum who was so soft. He was hard but fair. My dad had always warned me to never smoke, for if he ever caught me, he would break both my legs. Obviously, he was not really going to do that but I was likely to get 'a good hiding' as we would say.

One day I was standing down our street with a cigarette in my hand, trying to look like a hard man and smoke at the same time. Around the corner comes my dad and he walked right into me! I quickly moved my hand and cigarette into my coat pocket, but I was in that much of a panic I didn't have time to put the cigarette out!

When I think of it now, I do think, he had caught on that I had been smoking. Because while he smartly stood talking to me about things that didn't matter - I started to burn! My coat pocket started to smoke and I started shouting and throwing it out to the ground. My dad turned to me and said; "I'm away for a walk, I'll see you when I get back, now go you home." He walked off.

Dad taught me how to stand up for myself and very much wanted me to protect my family.

My younger brother Stephen would attend the Gospel Hall Sunday School and one day he arrived home badly hurt. Two of the lads had beaten him up in an alleyway. They were also sent to the Sunday school by their parents, as most of us were. My dad sat and listened to what took place and then he turned to me and said; "Next week you're going to Sunday school!" I argued that I wasn't going to no Sunday school but he said; "Yes you are, you will find out who these two boys are and when you come out of that hall, if you don't dig the two of them then I will dig you!" They never hit my brother again.

Give an account...

My dad always told me that it didn't matter if you get beat but you have to give an account of yourself, otherwise people will bully you. This was my dad's philosophy, to give a good account of yourself. He believed it wasn't the size of the dog in the fight but rather the size of the fight in the dog.

One school day, a boy bigger than me called James was goading me on. I was very small and skinny and he kept on and on at me. But then he said a derogatory thing about my mum and I snapped in the middle of class. So, I swung, kicked and thumped at him, getting the better of him but then the teacher ran in between us and broke it up.

I was walking away and felt a tap on the shoulder, thinking it was the teacher I turned around and all I saw was a flash and the student I'd been fighting had hit me another one. My eye closed over, it was bleeding badly.

When I came home my mum was so upset wanting to know what had happened. Shortly afterwards, my dad came in from work and saw me, he said; "Hold on a minute Violet, hold on." He asked me what had happened so I told him. My mum was so upset that I had got this injury because of her but dad turned to me and said; "Just right, don't you let anyone say that about your mummy again!" My mum was trying to comfort me but my dad was asking;

"Did you give a good account of yourself?" I said that I had so that was it, he told me to run on. That was just my dad all over.

Despite the difficulties, we were a very happy family, very close knit. We really loved each other. We didn't have much but we didn't want for anything. Our parents did their best to provide everything we needed. Even though most of the time we felt very unsafe and uncertain because of what was going on outside our door, I always felt safe and secure when I was inside with my parents as my dad was invincible to me.

Years later when he died, it nearly broke me, as to me it wasn't possible. I had to accept that my dad wasn't invincible and it hit me hard. I really miss him as he always had great wisdom, everyone looked to him for direction. He had a great strength about him, even when he was dying he battled death with dignity. He had my full admiration.

Chapter Three
The trouble begins...

In the summer of 1978, I used to hang out with an older guy we called Toast. His Granny's surname was French, so we called him French Toast.

One day, he said to me; "Ken do you want to make some money?"

I said, "Yes, of course!"

He said, "I have a great idea, let's take the lead off the factory roof and sell it!"

If you have ever watched some of those comedy films that has a break-in, that would have been like us. The factory was surrounded by rows of barbed wire in order to either get through or go over we tucked our trouser legs into our socks.

We found a low part in the wall and climbed carefully over the barbed wire entering a large forecourt. Climbing up the steps and then onto the roof of the building, we started to strip the lead off the roof.

With our lack of experience in stealing, when we rolled it all up it was far too heavy to carry. We looked around and climbed down a drain spout into the lower yard and there were yellow lorries with ladders on them. We looked for a wheelbarrow thinking that we could do a few runs and leave the lead in the back of one of the derelict houses as they were our playground then. This would keep it safe until we got it to the scrap merchant for our money. While we were looking for a wheelbarrow though we discovered a ladder which took us up to another roof, we climbed up and there was a pyramid-shaped skylight window. It was only lead-lined so we were able to peel the lead off and we lifted the glass panels out. We lifted up the ladder and dropped it down through the window and we ransacked the offices. We thought there might be some petty cash so we looked through everything for it. We filled our pockets with all sorts of things. We lifted what we could and climbed back up the ladder again and back to the yard. We were looking around for a wheelbarrow to put our rolls of lead into. We found a store which was full of equipment and tried to jimmy-open the small window. The window cracked but we got it open, I was only a wee skinny thing at the time so Toast told me to get inside and open some of the larger windows from the inside. The window was really tiny, I remember trying to squeeze in through the gap, only my head fitting. The next thing I remember was this big hand grabbing me from behind.

This big man had found us, he had me by one hand and Toast by the other. He pulled me out of the window. He marched us down the yard and locked us in the back of his car. He left us alone while he closed the main gates, as we watched him putting the bar on, Toast said to me; "When he gets in the driver's side, we are out the other side, okay?" I nodded. Then he whispered to me; "But wait till he gets into the car!" He got in and as soon as he closed the door, we jumped out the other side!

We ran up through the back alleyways, we were running so hard and all I can remember was the thuds of this big man chasing us. Toast of course was way ahead of me with him being older, he had more speed. I could hear the noise of the big man's boots closing in on me and then I could hear him panting. The next thing I knew, this big hand grabbed me and I was caught. He dragged me back with the collar of my shirt of which I was nearly choked to death, but he didn't care, he was not letting go this time!

By the time he dragged me back to his car, the police had arrived with dogs. There were Land Rovers all over the place, the whole street was out. My older sister, Elaine was there and when she saw me she went crazy, she started pulling at this tall man telling him to leave her brother alone! This time they threw me in the back of one of the police Land Rovers and took me to the station. I was only eleven at the time.

They didn't catch Toast and despite them keeping me and questioning me for hours, I wouldn't give him up. I didn't tell them who was with me. Even the police were amazed at this wee boy, so young, wouldn't give up his mate. It ended up eventually through social services that Toast was caught. Our fingerprints were over everything so they got him identified through time. I think we got up to this mischief simply out of boredom.

As an outcome, I had to register with the police station twice a week for a period of time. They decided not to prosecute but I had to agree to visits from social workers. They came and visited every week and took notes on what I was doing, who I was with etc.

Stealing beer...

My mates and I used to get up to all sorts of mischief and one of our favourite things to do was to steal beer. There were rows of derelict houses where we lived so we used to steal kegs of beer and roll them up the railway lines that were at the bottom of our street. We would break into the local pub and take a keg of beer at a time.

Most of us in Northern Ireland would remember the Maine man. He did his rounds and nearly everyone on the street bought the Maine lemonade. He came around every Saturday, so every time there were bottles sitting out for collection. We would have lifted a couple each, brought them round to this old house and fill them with beer.

The first time we stole a beer keg we couldn't figure out how to get the beer out!

We borrowed hammers and all sorts but couldn't break into the steel drum. We were stuck as we didn't know what to do with it, we certainly couldn't take it back! Then I had a bright idea, there was a man at the end of the street that ran a garage, he did vehicle repairs. I thought, if we could get a blowtorch, then we could blow a hole in it!

So we went down to the garage and climbed on the roof. It was only a corrugated roof, there were some bolts loose so I was able to slide the sheets across. I dropped down into the garage and saw a small handheld blowtorch, I lifted it and headed back to the beer. We looked at it and hadn't a clue how to start it, we got matches and it started up. We blew two holes in the keg and we emptied the beer. The beer was flat but we drank it anyway.

Rebelling...

I remember trying to be a man before my time at fourteen asking my dad if I could get tattoos, he told me that he would kill me if I came home with one! I decided to get my first tattoo anyway and off I went to the local tattoo parlour in Tigers Bay. Now if you know what Belfast was like in those days, a tattoo parlour in this case was a guy's living room, and the guy with the tattoo gun wanted to practise so I decided to give it a go! He was no artist and the tattoos were that bad, I always keep them covered now but at the time I thought I was cool. I tried to hide them from my parents but someone had told my dad what I had been up to, so he slapped my arm one day deliberately and I yelled sore! He asked me what was wrong as he had only, according to him, lightly tapped me, so I tried to pretend it was okay but the pain was intense. He asked to see my arm. I knew I had been rattled.

Just shortly after I had got found out with my tattoos, I was in more trouble. At night-time, I used to sneak out of the house and stay in the dark away from lights until I would arrive at the home bakery at the end of the street. It had an old sash window in the bakery that slid up and down and we knew there were only two wooden blocks that held the window at the top so we could pull these out and open the window. We would climb through the window into the bakery and switch on the ovens and heat the sausage rolls in the middle of the night. After we ate our fill we would steal their buns and whatever was left, we used for bun fights! Obviously through time the bakery caught on that we were getting in somehow and we didn't know, but the police had found fingerprints and we were arrested. As crafty as I was, I told the police that my mate's Grandad used to clean the bakery and sometimes we would have gone with him to help him clean it. This explained my fingerprints being there so they had to let me go!

Getting stoned...

In my youth, I became a young Mod. Back then that was the whole rage. There were the skinheads and the Mod's. I preferred the Mod's as I liked their style. I wore my green parka, bowling shoes and my two-tone trousers. I even got a Vespa scooter eventually.

One day, I was over in the park, we were all drinking and we used to go the Grove Community Centre, everyone knew it as Sid's Disco. We were out drinking all this beer we had. There was a wine lodge, owned by a man called Eric. He used to make his own concoction in a wooden barrel. He would then fill the lemonade bottles up for us. It was called Eric's home brew, otherwise known as Rocket Fuel! Somebody brought some Rocket Fuel to the park one day and we drank it, the next thing I can remember was my dad and my uncle Trevor carrying me by the hands and feet like I was a dead animal!

While I had been drinking, my mate's brother had ran and got my dad, he told him to go quickly to the park as I had been stoned by the skinheads!

My dad came running as he thought the skinheads had physically attacked me but he was trying to hide what I had done, by blaming the skinheads for getting me stoned. So my dad brought my uncle thinking that I was in the middle of a riot but then he found me lying on the ground, out for the count.

I remember he was so angry with me when he brought me home. He sat me down in the house and said; "Do you want a drink son?" I said; "No, I have had plenty!"

He was cross, he said; "You want a drink, I'll give you a drink!" He lifted a bottle of whiskey and started emptying it down my throat! Then I vomited.

He threw me up to bed. I must have slept for a while but I remember getting up from the bed and going over to the window, we had a long window with a small opening at the top. I was afraid to leave my bedroom so I vomited out of the opening and it ran down the whole window. The next day, I was wakened by this squeaking noise. It was my dad standing out on the roof, washing the window. I saw him looking in so I got up and closed the blinds quickly as I knew he was going to kill me!

Chapter Four
It's a knockout!...

My dad wanted me to try and do something to stop me getting into trouble so I started boxing and training. I really enjoyed it but after boxing for a little while, I started suffering from migraines and the doctor wanted me to stop so it hindered me a bit. I wanted to continue fighting but because of the severity of the headaches, I was on an early bed routine, a no dairy diet and painkillers when needed. The migraines didn't improve so the doctor banned me from boxing.

It was the Friday after school at the beginning of March, 1983 when I was just 16 years old, that my Granny said to me; "Kenneth, I was looking through the paper and I saw a job for an apprentice upholsterer." I was surprised and didn't know why she was telling me about it, but she continued; "I rang about it for you as you need a job."

I said to her; "Granny, I am at school!" When my dad came home from work, she spoke to him and he agreed. An hour later, this man arrives at our home. He introduced himself as Andy Maguire. He said to me; "I believe you are looking for a job?"

I said; "No."

My dad interrupted; "Yes he is!" "I am at school, I don't leave till June." I cried.

Andy replied; "Well, I need you now."

Dad said; "Never worry about waiting to June, if you can get a job you are leaving now!"

Andy turned to me and asked me what I wanted to do? I never got to answer.

My dad asked; "When can he start?" Andy said he wanted someone for Monday morning, this was Friday evening. My dad said; "Right, he will be there on Monday morning."

That was it, decision was made. I was forced out of school with no qualifications. My first job was as a general dogsbody, stripping cloth off old suites and helping with deliveries. It wasn't enjoyable but I was earning an income. When I was about eighteen, I got heavily into sport again. My brother Stephen and my sister's future husband, William and I, started training in Loughside Leisure Centre. We did kick-boxing and as we got better we started to compete all around the island of Ireland.

During that time, I won an Irish title at lightweight then at light welterweight and a Northern Ireland welterweight also. I was quite successful, winning lots of trophies and prizes for fighting. But in 1989 I went over to Oldham and fought for the British title. When I came home, I was suffering migraines again, just a repeat of what happened when I was younger. I attended a neurologist in the Royal Victoria Hospital in Belfast. I got brain scans and they advised me to stop fighting. I didn't want to give it up so I continued on and I fought for the All-Ireland welterweight championships and at that fight, a guy I should have beaten easily ended up winning as every time he hit me I was frightened about what was going on in my brain. I knew during that fight that I would have to give it up as now I was too paranoid about the damage I was doing whereas before, it wouldn't have cost me a thought.

I stopped fighting and I went and did my IABA (Irish Amateur Boxing Association) Coaching Course. I started coaching young boxers in The White City/Midland Boxing Club. I enjoyed coaching but I missed the competitiveness of fighting. I had still always been weight training, just for building strength. I started getting more into body building rather than weight training. I did what I could naturally, then I was introduced to anabolic steroids, other guys were using them and I could see the gains they were getting.

Getting high...

I got a job as a bouncer at a night club in Belfast, where fights were common most nights. Through this position as part of a team, I got to know of shortcuts to increase muscle mass quickly. It was then I was introduced to injecting anabolic steroids which later led to drugs and to the addiction of them.

One night I threw a guy out of the club for causing trouble. The guy shouted back at me; "I am going to shoot you!"

I said; "Away you go!" About half an hour later, a car pulled up in the side street next to the club, the guy gets out with a gun. I saw him coming and slammed the large iron door. He kicked the door but knew he was not getting through and jumped back into the car and they drove off. I did a few nights after that but decided the job was not worth the risk. Even in leaving the job, I was still hooked to ecstasy. I thought I controlled it, but it actually was controlling me, I became addicted. Some nights I took five tablets, others up to ten tablets, whatever I could afford and they wouldn't have knocked me out but they knocked me out of my senses.

Quickly I was spiralling into debt due to the cravings for ecstasy, anything I could sell was sold cheap to try and gather money to feed the addiction. It now got to the stage, I couldn't pay my rent any more. The landlord had me evicted from his house and I ended up on the street. I was homeless.

During the time I was a bouncer, I also drove a lorry but my health and all was going downhill and one day the foreman, called me to the side and said; "Kenny, what's wrong?" I told him I couldn't go on any more. He said; "Kenny, I used to be an alcoholic and you know what happened to me?"

I was shocked at this revelation, I said; "No, what?" He said; "The Lord Jesus Christ came into my life and saved me."

Well, I swore at that man, I was really mad at him! I cursed him up and down and told him where to go. I just didn't care about anything and it was not long after that I lost the job due to being so unreliable.

Suicide...

Homeless and jobless, I stayed in friend's houses for a while, just sleeping on sofas where I could get in. I had no money and no prospects, I was just living for the next high. After a while of sleeping rough, I got upgraded as a mate of mine offered me his spare room with a mattress. For several months I slept on a mattress that lay directly on bare floorboards with nothing else, not a sheet or a pillow. But at least I was dry when I slept! I did not realise then, internally I was becoming so depressed, I became suicidal. I heard voices in my head, telling me that my life was over and I wanted life to be over. It was terrible.

I was so bad on drugs, one night at a party I started to hallucinate and I saw people turning into demons right in front of me. I was terrified! Someone had spiked my drink and I collapsed. I woke up in a hedge a few streets away. They obviously thought I had died so they dumped me away from the house. When I came around, I got myself out of the hedge and made my way back to the party. I was still that far out of my mind, I could not distinguish which room was what. Even standing looking into a bathroom I asked a mate; "Is this the bathroom?" I had lost all sense of reality.

Death threats...

To get some money and feed my drug addiction, I used to do some taxi work. During that time, I had three attempts on my life from paramilitaries. I was almost shot on three occasions; twice by loyalist paramilitaries and once by the IRA.

On the first occasion, I was driving a taxi. On the Sunday I was asked to pick up someone in a bar in a well-known IRA area. The bars were all closed on Sundays but there were a few that you could get in the back door. None of the taxi firms would go into this estate but ours. I pulled up and these two guys got in and said they wanted to go to the docks. I knew there was a bar down there that opened on a Sunday so thought nothing of it. On route they questioned me, wanted to know who I was, asked me if I was Protestant or Catholic, lots of different things. They asked who I knew from the estate so I said that I knew nobody.

They told me they were the IRA and they knew who I was and that I was going to be shot.

When we arrived at the docks there was another man there to meet them, he was dressed in black. They told me that he was going to shoot me.

The Friday night before I had happened to pick up two well-known guys who actually owned a bar in an IRA area. I remembered their names, where they lived etc. so I said to the men; "I know a mate of yours..." And said his name.

They looked at each other and one of them asked me; "How do you know him?"

I said; "Oh a mate of mine lives up beside him, see him all the time."

One of them got out of the car to speak to the man in black and the other sat in behind my seat. He told me not to move. I didn't look around, I just sat there. I knew he was sitting directly behind me, he said; "Don't move or I will shoot you." Then the guy who had left the car, came back down the alleyway and he seemed cross, he got back into the car and told me to drive them back to the estate. I thought then that they mustn't want to shoot me here so they must be taking me back to the estate to shoot me. I didn't want to die so I was trying to figure how to get away.

Even as I was driving back from the docks I queried if I should just drive off the motorway, if I was going to die, I might as well take them with me?! However, I drove on, as per their request and returned to the estate. I drove up to the bar and as I swung in towards the building I could see a few guys standing behind the bar in the waste ground. One of the guys in the car pointed for them to go into the estate out of the road, the other one leant into me and said; "You open your mouth and you are dead! Now take yourself off." They got out of the car and I didn't waste any time, I drove off quickly. I reported it to my boss, he phoned down and warned that the taxi firm wouldn't be covering the estate any more but the IRA disowned it. It was well organised but thankfully I survived. It scared the life out of me, I thought I was a goner. Because my name is the same as my dad's they probably thought they had someone from the UDR.

Then I remember the second time it happened to me, I was in our local club. A mate of mine was a soldier and he started dating this girl who was an ex-partner of a paramilitary. News had got back to him that his 'missus' was dating someone else.

I was sitting one night having a drink and these boys came over and said; "Ken, we want to talk to you out the back." In the bar there was a room at the back with one door in and one door out. It consisted of a small bar and a table. I went though and sat down, they questioned me. "Where were you on Saturday night?" One of them asked me.

I said; "I was in Newtownards." He mentioned this guy's name to me and said; "You were with his wife in here on Saturday night making fun of him!"

I said; "What? No, I was in Newtownards on Saturday night." I denied it, it wasn't me. I knew it was my mate they were looking for but didn't know why they thought it was me.

They told me that they had sent a team away to get the gear as they were going to shoot me. I said; "Why?"

The guy started to get angry, he said; "Because he is one of our men and you are making fun of him, that's why!"

I wasn't though as I was in Newtownards on Saturday night but they wouldn't listen.

He said to me; "Have yourself a pint there and forget it." He set me down a pint in front of me and started playing a game of pool. This was my farewell drink.

My mate Geordie walked into the club and through to the back room where I was, a couple of the guys tried to stand in the doorway to block him. Geordie was looking at me, he was obviously trying to work out what was going on.

The guy started shouting at him; "Geordie, out – out!" But Geordie stood his ground and shouted at me; "Alright Ken, what's going on?" They were jostling back and forward, they were arguing but they pushed him out back into the club. About ten minutes later, they came back into me and said; "Right Ken, away you go!"

I said; "I thought you were going to shoot me?"

And they said; "Well, we heard that you were in Newtownards - Geordie told us."

So I went back into the club and asked Geordie what had happened. He told me that they said to him that I was running around with this man's wife. Of course he knew it wasn't me so was able to vouch for me thankfully. Geordie knew I was in Newtownards on Saturday night as I happened to call in to visit him afterwards. So whenever they had spoken to him, Geordie's response was: "Sure Ken wasn't even here on Saturday night, he was in Newtownards!"

So they said to him; "Oh this fella must be telling us the truth!"

They let me go. They then went back to the other guy and a whole row started that they had been given the wrong information.

Just a few months later, I was at a club and I was put under threat that I was going to be shot again for the same reasons. When the club was finishing they told me to stay behind. When the club was clear I saw two guys that I had known from my childhood, they came over and asked me what was up? I explained about the mix-up before and they said that nothing happened without their say-so. They told me to go on, that nothing would be happening to me. I knew they were high up in the UVF, they weren't sanctioning anything so I was again, free to go.

When under threat, look to the Lord...

1 Samuel 27:1; *'And David said in his heart, I shall now perish one day by the hand of Saul: there is nothing better for me than that I should speedily escape into the land of the Philistines; and Saul shall despair of me, to seek me any more in any coast of Israel: so shall I escape out of his hand.'*

We learn in this passage that David had a perceived threat on his life. While he was absolutely right about the danger he was in, the death threat was very real, yet he had allowed his fear to overcome his faith. He had allowed his worry to overcome the Word and his panic to overcome the promises of God. David knew in his heart, once a thought, a word, a threat or a lie reaches the heart then that's where the real problem starts to lay hold over us, take root in us and bear fruit from us and that is for the good or the bad.

We can decide to become either victim or victor, under condemnation or an overcomer as we allow the words of life to enter our heart, or words of death. As it says in Proverbs 18:21; *'Death and life are in the power of the tongue: and they that love it shall eat the fruit thereof.'*

We must be careful not only how we hear, but how we speak to others, about others and over others. We must also reject the falsehood and lying negativity of bitter spirits being employed by the devil to slow us down, hold us back and quench our faith in the promise and provision of God's word in our lives. David was chosen of God, anointed by Samuel the prophet and was in the training ground of life, being tried by the natural and the spiritual, the temporal and the eternal to prepare him for the greater plan and purpose of God in his life. Yet he allowed stinking-thinking and negative noise to enter his heart through his ear gate and it caused him to become weary.

Proverbs 12:25; *'Heaviness in the heart of man maketh it stoop: but a good word maketh it glad.'*

A stooping heart or a glad heart! Which one is better, which one is yours?

David said in his heart, that he would now perish one day at the hand of Saul. What we need to learn from this, is that whether it's a threat of death from an illness, a disease, an evil report or the slaying of your character falsely, we must never make the hasty and rash decision to trust our own feelings and thoughts, neither should we place our soul in the hands of another, outside of Christ and His Word. What should you do then?

Here are some Scriptures to remember.

Psalm 105:3; *'Glory ye in his holy name: let the heart of them rejoice that seek the Lord.'*

Isaiah 57:15; *'For thus saith the high and lofty One that inhabiteth eternity, whose name is Holy; I dwell in the high and holy place, with him also that is of a contrite and humble spirit, to revive the spirit of the humble, and to revive the heart of the contrite ones.'*

Notice. Glory in Him. Seek Him and you'll find, He's with you. His Word is forever settled and His promises remain. He is with you to revive you in times of despair and need, so don't fear but have faith as Jesus said in Mark 5:36; *'Be not afraid, only believe.'* Place your all in Him, His Word, His promises and His faithfulness, nothing shall separate you from the love of God which is in Christ Jesus our Lord. (Romans 8).

As we read in 1 Samuel 27:1; *'David said in his heart.'* It's important to learn from this, don't trust your own heart but entrust your heart to the heart of your Father in Heaven. David in the next breath says; *'I will now perish one day by the hand of Saul.'* Now while me must be wise, and while we must be cautious of things which come into our lives, we must stop, pause, and take a moment. Most times we allow ourselves to get into a panic or a tailspin and become unnerved, stressed and ill over a situation. Many tend to lose out on God's benefits and blessings of that day because they're too obsessed with the enemy's threat, that they become consumed by it. Christian... don't lose out on life today by worrying about tomorrow!

Matthew 6:34; *'Take therefore no thought for the morrow: for the morrow shall take thought for the things of itself. Sufficient unto the day is the evil thereof.'*

In 1 Samuel 27:1 we read; *'... there is nothing better for me...'*

Here is another lie which entered David's heart. How subtle is the enemy to simply plant a seed and what we constantly think, helps it to grow. The seed of fear kills the fruit of faith.

What is fear? Fear can be healthy and unhealthy. A healthy fear tells us to look both ways while crossing the road, while unhealthy fear tells us never to cross the road.

Fear as I believe it is... **False Evidence Appearing Real!**

1 Samuel 27:1; *'...there is nothing better for me that I should speedily escape into the hands of the Philistines.'* WHAT? Why would we let fear drive us into the hands of our enemy? Let disillusionment and disappointment take you into the world and land of the ungodly and destroy your witness and testimony? Far off fields are not what you think, in reality they are not as green and pleasant as they look from where you are.

David ran in haste to the enemy thinking things would be better, but listen to what the Scripture says in 1 Samuel 21:12; *'And David laid up these words in his heart, and was sore afraid of Achish the king of Gath.'* David ran from Saul afraid, but became sore afraid of Achish the Philistine king. Christian, if you are ever going to run, run to Jesus, trust in His Word and hold on to His promises!

Colossians 3:16; *'Let the word of Christ dwell in you richly in all wisdom; teaching and admonishing one another in psalms and hymns and spiritual songs, singing with grace in your hearts to the Lord.'*

'Finally, brethren, whatsoever things are true, whatsoever things are honest, whatsoever things are just, whatsoever things are pure, whatsoever things are lovely, whatsoever things are of good report; if there be any virtue, and if there be any praise, think on these things.' Philippians 4:8.

Section 2

When all Hope is Gone

'Now the God of hope fill you with all joy and peace in believing, that ye may abound in hope, through the power of the Holy Ghost.'

Romans 15:13

Chapter Five
Time to jump...

Just before I was evicted from Mineral Street, just off York Road in Belfast, my mental health was very poor. To be honest, I think my mind was going. I remember seeing shadows on the walls, and every time I glanced at my wardrobe which sat at the bottom of my bed, somehow my mind was showing me, it was my coffin. It really freaked me out.

One day, I just couldn't cope any more with it, so I climbed out onto a window ledge. As I was standing there in the cold air, I heard voices telling me to 'jump, jump, jump,' as if they were going to a beat of a drum. It was very real. The voices were convincing me, if I jumped it would be all over, they went on and on until I couldn't take it any more.

Then another voice spoke; "What about your mum, what about your family?"

It was just back and forward between these evil voices and this reasoning voice. I remember looking down from the roof and thinking; "What if I didn't kill myself, what if I just broke my legs?' That would be even worse!

I remember stepping off the ledge onto the roof and crying; "God if you are there, help me!" I was so broken but God didn't respond, did He even hear me?

I was being haunted. I was terrified and I really dreaded night time coming. My friend Gary, would have walked me home many a night. When he had to leave I would have freaked out. I couldn't cope with being on my own. Fear would have gripped me like a vice.

One day, I was lying in a friend's house on a bed and the wind was really beating the rain against the window. It was raining really hard. I couldn't see or hear anything but I sensed there was something there, something downstairs. My heart started to race, I kept wondering, is there somebody downstairs? Then I felt that something was coming up the stairs towards me! It was very silent, there were no creaks or any noise but I knew it was there and it came into the room I was in. Again, I was thinking, this is in my head as I wasn't sure what was real any more. I couldn't see anything but there was a real sense of darkness came over me, a real evil. I rolled over on the bed unto my back and the only way I can explain it, it was like something entered into me. It was a bit like when someone grabs the lapel on your jacket and shakes you. I felt like I had been grabbed but it wasn't my flesh, it was my spirit it had grabbed and lifted me out of my body. It was pure evil, real satanic.

I know many Christians who will read this part will find it difficult to accept maybe this took place, but I experienced it. As much as God is real, the devil and his hordes also seek to be real. I remember coming out like a crab's bend, that is the best way I can describe it. As if I had been pulled by the chest out. I felt myself leaving my body. This evil presence had me, it was as if it was breathing on me. It shook me. Then it threw me and I ended up back in my body again. The fear I had at night time because of the things I had experienced was nothing compared to this. It was unimaginable. There was so much fear, it is hard to explain. It was just horrific. I knew this thing was real, this thing was pure evil. Whatever it was, it wasn't an hallucination, I knew this thing was there. I saw myself leave my body and it wasn't like looking down on myself, I was looking upwards. I just seemed to be outside of myself. I remember thinking, I'm going to go to hell, hell is coming to get me.

That was the first night I truly turned to God. I cried onto Him; "God help me, please help me!" As I cried out to God, the rain stopped beating against the window. Everything went quiet and calm. The evil presence had gone!

There were so many times during my drug addiction that I said to counsellors; if only I could flick a switch. I just wanted to switch it all off so I could change, that it would be all over. Well, for that brief moment, it was like somebody had flicked a switch. There was calm, there was peace. For the first time in my life, I felt peace within myself.

I sat up on the bed, I looked around me and said aloud; "I am going insane, I am going insane!" And just like that, in a flash, the dark presence was back! I remember being petrified, I couldn't move. It was like I was pinned to the bed. I realised these things were very real.

Sign posts...

The next day, I was straight down to the pub. I was sitting with my two mates. I was telling them what had happened. Paul said to me; "You need to go to church!"

"I'm not going to church!" I scoffed.

Paul said; "I'll go with you."

I laughed at him, I said; "Big lad, you've lost your head more than I have!"

And I didn't go and things got worse for about three months or so until one Friday a family member was in court and I went to give them moral support. Entering the court house, I threatened the opposing side, warning them that I was going to kill them! They started yelling at me; "What have I done, don't be attacking me!" This alerted the officials and they were going to take me for contempt of court but because it was not in the court room, they let me go with a warning.

Later I went to a club and on my way to it, I had taken drugs so I was out of my head. Some guy started fighting with me in the club, and as I was standing up to him, Stephen, my brother, who was with me, caught on that there was a coach-load of them, he shouted at me; "You are going to get us killed!" So we exited the club quietly and got a taxi to another party.

When we arrived at the party, we met some of the girls from the street we grew up in. They asked me about an old mutual friend of ours that I hadn't saw in a while. They told me they had become 'good living.'

I said; "Yes, I heard."

Then they all turned to me and said; "Would you ever think of turning good living?"

"No, I would not! Catch yourself on!" I laughed.

We left the party early the next morning and as Stephen and I were walking down the road, I remember, it was a very bright day, yet things inside of me had got so dark. What did I have to live for? I had decided that I was going to finish myself off that morning. I started talking to my brother, I said; "Stephen, don't mess your life up."

He said to me; "You are talking funny, why are you talking like that?"

I left Stephen and walked into a mate's house, my plan was to raid the medicine cabinet. Take whatever pills I could find and finish it. I found what I wanted, though I can't really remember what happened to me. I just remember when I came round, I was lying on the floor. My face was swollen, all puffed up and I could hardly see out of my eyes, they were like slits. My plan to finish it all hadn't worked. My body was in agony but stranger than that, I could make out silhouettes of people with me. Standing over me was Eddie and Margaret Anderson. They were a Christian couple who had been praying for me. They said to each other; "He's coming round!"

Then the next thing they said; "Do you want to go to church?"

All I could think of was; 'Do you want to get me an ambulance?!'

Chapter Six
Meeting the Lord...

I am not sure if I blanked out again or what happened but the next thing I remember, I was dressed in a suit and sitting in their car on the way to a church. They were driving me to Whitewell Tabernacle Church in Belfast.

When we arrived, everyone was greeting each other in the car park and I was thinking; 'What on earth am I doing here?'

Voices in my head were demanding me; "Don't go in, don't go in!"

I remember saying to Eddie; "I'll go to the Tudor Lodge pub across the road, sure I will see you when you come out."

He said; "You are here now, come on ahead, you said you would come."

As I sat within the main church, I was looking around and the voices started ridiculing everyone around me, they were calling them every name and being very explicit in the names. The service began and the people were praising, lifting their hands and singing their hearts out and all I could think of was; 'Look at these gimps!'

I just wanted to get out! I said to Eddie; "I need to go!" But, I was stuck, they had me sitting in the middle of a row with numerous people sitting on both sides of me. I started to feel really anxious, I just wanted to get out. The choir sang and then Pastor McConnell got up and preached. I was shocked with the passion he preached with. I knew he believed what he was saying. I admired his devotion, I thought to myself as I listened to every word. He preached about the obstacles God puts in our way to stop us going to hell. He started talking about different obstacles. Obstacles being the witness in work, the tract in the town given by a Christian, hearing about the love of God for you, forgiveness, healing, grace and mercy. I was shown pictures in my mind of these people who had crossed my path in many a dark season, who had witnessed, sharing the saving grace of God through Christ. Like a filing cabinet in my head, scene after scene was flashing before me. God loved me so much he put these obstacles in the sinner's road to hell.

I thought, has the preacher got it wrong? Surely, we are all going to heaven and it's the devil who is placing obstacles on my way to heaven, but no, Pastor McConnell then preached the last, final and the ultimate obstacle of God's great love is Calvary. He preached Jesus Christ and Him crucified and I saw Jesus taking my place and I was totally transfixed on Him.

The more he preached, the more I said; 'That happened to me.' I looked suspiciously at the people with me and wondered; 'Did they tell him I was coming here?'

Pastor McConnell continued on; "Now, tonight you are here and you are at the greatest obstacle of your life." He then preached Christ and the cross.

I met the Lord at the foot of the cross as an altar call was made; "Is there a young man or a young woman here who is not saved but you know you need to be?" I knew he was speaking to me but who told him I was coming? Little did I know God was convicting me and dealing with me. Calvary was etched on my mind and burning into my soul. "Let me see your hand if you want Jesus to save you!" He said.

I said to myself; "God, I have nothing to offer you, my body is wrecked. I'm without hope, with no money, no strength, no home to go to, I come with nothing, but if you take me and save me, I will serve you all my days." I prayed and cried unto the Lord and He heard me.

I said; "God you know I have nothing to give you here." My body was broken, my life was in bits. I was no use to Him. "If you can do anything with this it's yours and I will serve you."

I threw my hand up and after the service made my way to the Magee room, within the church building. I could hardly walk, I was all over the place. The sweat was pouring off me, my heart was getting faster and faster. All I could think was; "Oh yeah God, I told you I would give you everything and now you are going to kill me!"

When I went inside the room, the sweat was dripping off the end of my nose, even off my fingers. The heat was unreal. I started crying my eyes out and then I panicked as I said to myself; "My Dad will kill me if he finds me like this!"

I didn't know if I was taking a panic attack or what was happening. I was shaking. One of the men, said to me; "Don't worry, sometimes this happens."

I looked at him and I cried; "What is happening, what is happening?"

He said; "Son, the Lord is just dealing with you." I told him that I was on drugs and drink and he said; "Don't worry, the Lord is just wringing you out!" He prayed with me and when he did, everything just settled. It was like I was carrying a really heavy, dark rucksack on my back and I just threw it off.

I knew when leaving that room, I was different. I knew something had happened to me. I felt so light, like I was walking on giant marshmallows. As the Bible says; *'Come unto me, all ye that labour and are heavy laden, and I will give you rest.'* Matthew 11:28

Afterwards, I walked across the foyer and towards the doors I first came in, where the voices had warned me against it. This time I didn't hear those voices, instead I heard the voice of Pastor McConnell. In his sermon he said; "You go out those doors tonight without Christ and you could go out into a lost eternity." I heard that again as I reached the doors.

These were the same doors that the devil tried to stop me using, he nearly drove me insane earlier. I stopped dead at the doors and a flash of fear came over me, I just thought to myself; "A lost eternity? Not tonight I won't!"

I pushed the doors and went outside into the car park to find Eddie. It was the greatest high I had ever experienced. The high of God! I felt freer than ever before. Eddie shook my hand and said; "Good to know you, Ken."

I said; "Sure, you do know me!"

"Yes, but not as my brother!" He drove me to a friend's house and that night I was tested. I was lying on the living room floor thinking through everything that had happened. Just suddenly, this tall dark shadow stood over me. It was really tall, it stood about 8-9 foot over me. I instantly recognised the presence, I knew this was the thing that came to me before and lifted me. I turned my face around to the wall and I said; "Lord Jesus, you know I meant everything I said to you. I am yours and you are mine - I surrender myself to you." Immediately, the presence disappeared.

The next day I was walking down the Shore road. I was walking past Seaview Presbyterian church where they have cherry blossom trees. The cherry blossoms had come off and were laying on the ground, there was a vapour coming up from the ground and I could smell them. Before this, my senses were all dead but now for the first time in a long time, I could smell again. I was hearing car tyres on the road, I was also seeing things for the first time, I was noticing street signs that I didn't even know were there before. Everything was heightened. I felt like I was alive.

As I walked down the road, I felt like I was able to lift my head up. I passed Fortwilliam Gospel Hall and I noticed this huge sign, it had been there for years but today I saw it for the first time, as a Christian. It said; "Prepare to meet thy God." As I saw it, I just knew - I am prepared now. I am ready! I walked on down to the Metropolitan Tabernacle and went into the restaurant where the pastors were having a cup of tea. I walked in through the door and yelled; "I got saved last night!" Pastor McConnell jumped to his feet and came over; "What was that son? You got saved?"

I said; "Yes!"

"Was this last night? What happened?" He asked.

I said; "I have been addicted to alcohol and drugs..." Pastor McConnell interrupted me, shouting at everyone; "Listen everyone, listen boys!" And he said; "Tell us what happened?"

I said; "I got saved last night." Everyone congregated around me.

Pastor McConnell said; "Isn't that fantastic!" They were all delighted.

On the third day...

Three days after coming to know the Lord, I had this awful attack of temptation. I didn't know what to do so I thought I would go down to the church as in my naivety, I thought that must be where Jesus is. I walked down and Pastor Shaw Higgins greeted me, he prayed with me and I remember they had given me a tiny blue New Testament and Psalms Bible. I had kept it in the zip pocket of my bomber jacket's sleeve so I would take it everywhere with me. He said to me; "Ken, you just keep praising and trusting and get into some Christian fellowship." We prayed and I felt much better.

I left and as I was walking up the road, I met a guy I knew.

He said; "Well Ken, where are you for? Were you out at the weekend?"

I said; "Yeah, I was at church!"

He said; "You what?" This guy was a backslider.

I said to him; "I was at church and I got saved at the weekend."

He was delighted for me. I continued on up the road and it's funny how these things happen. The devil came alongside me in the form of a drug dealer. This was the guy that I used to phone and he would have met me wherever I was to get me my next high. He pulled up in his car next to the pavement and shouted at me; "Ken, you should see the stuff I'll have for this weekend! Give me a shout and let me know where you are going!"

I said; "I'm not going to need them!"

He said; "Why, who are you dealing with now?"

I said; "Nobody, I am not dealing with anybody."

He said; "Well, where are you going to get your gear?"

I told him; "I am not going to need it."

He looked so confused, he said; "What are you talking about?"

So I just told him about my salvation, I said; "I got saved at the weekend."

He laughed, he said to me; "Oh what are you up to?"

I said; "I am not up to anything, I got saved at the weekend."

He let a few expletives out and he said; "I'll see you at the weekend!"

I said; "Don't hold your breath!" And off he went.

At that time, the more people I told about my salvation, the stronger I became. As it says in Romans 10:9-12; *'That if thou shalt confess with thy mouth the Lord Jesus, and shalt believe in thine heart that God hath raised him from the dead, thou shalt be saved. For with the heart man believeth unto righteousness; and with the mouth confession is made unto salvation. For the scripture saith, Whosoever believeth on him shall not be ashamed. For there is no difference between the Jew and the Greek: for the same Lord over all is rich unto all that call upon him.'*

The more I told, the more my witness went out. People all over the place were saying; "We'll give him a week." Or, "He must be up to something." Or that I had simply just lost the plot! Obviously I had lost it but I had found sanity in Christ. I continued to grow in my walk with the Lord and was doing really well.

Unfortunately, though just around that time, my dear mum took ill. At first we didn't know what was wrong with her but in that December she was diagnosed as having an inoperable brain tumour. My mum would have went on odd occasions to the Presbyterian church but she wasn't a Christian.

I got myself a job and started working. After work I went down to see her at night. Not really knowing what I was doing but I used to sit and read the Scriptures with her then I prayed with her. I was really worried about my mum, I had a real sense that I was about to enter a really dark season in my life. Sometimes when things go wrong in our lives, we analyse them. We search out a reason 'why.' We usually find that we cannot work it out, we can't understand it, the answer eludes us. Frustration can set in and our hurts, our problems, our trials just seem to overshadow us. We feel like we can't go on any more. What do we do when it all goes wrong?

I remember when I was at school we had a maths book and at the very back of it were the answers. We used to think that our teacher was really silly as he obviously didn't know the answers were all there. So I used to go to the question and just write 'equals' then inserted the answer from the back. I never had such an easy time before doing my homework. Until one day the teacher said; "Davidson, come up and explain to me what you have done here?"

So I said to him; "Well there's the question and there's the answer."

He said; "Do you think I don't know that the answers are at the back of the book? It was the working out between the question and the answer that was your homework!"

It was the working out of the 'in between' that is what I had to learn, that is what I had to answer. That is the part I had to work out for myself, that is what I had to put into action to see come to pass. Here is the question, here is the problem. Now here is the answer but what is the process in between? Maybe your life is like that and you are in between. Are you in between problem and problem? You know the answer is that the Lord will bring you through, but right now you are in the working out of it. That's the hard bit isn't it. That's the part where you dig deep, where you keep trusting. That's the bit where you need fellowship.

Sometimes you wonder how did it all go wrong and how you will ever recover and how things will ever change. And how circumstances will be different. You wonder how you've let the Lord down or query will the Lord even forgive you? All these things go through the human mind. We're all wondering; "Lord where are you at times when things are happening?" When loved ones are sick and you feel like you have lost all hope, you don't know where to turn to. You don't know what to do. Everything seems amiss.

You know reader, in all of our lives, either people are in a valley, people are going through a valley, people are coming out the end or others are just entering the valley.

A conveyor-belt Christian experience is that we live either outside, going into, through or out the other end of different things in our lives. Sometimes we wonder, is there any light at the end of the tunnel? Is there any hope at the end of this situation? Where do we go from here, what do we do in the midst of it?

Sometimes we have to really dig deep, trust in the Lord and let Him bring us through. In Psalm 121:8, we read; *'The Lord shall preserve thy going out and thy coming in from this time forth, and even for evermore.'* Even in the valley, you are blessed. You might not think it and you might not feel like it or experience it but in the troubled times, you are blessed. God is good all the time. God isn't just good when you are out of the valley and on the mountain.

He isn't just good when you come through a circumstance or a situation, He is good ALL the time. In the valley of tears, even the valley of the shadow of death when the valley hangs over the one entering into it and those loved ones in mourning passing through it. Scripture refers; *'When we are in the valley, passing through the valley of Baca. (tears) He is with us.'* (Psalm 84:6).

David said; *'Yea, when I walk through the valley of the shadow of death, I will fear no evil,'* Psalm 23:4. Then He looks towards God and he says; *'For thou art with me.'*

The Lord Jesus is *'the lily of the valleys.'* (Song of Solomon 2:1) Notice the plural. In other words, He is your lily in your valley and He is my lily in my valley. He can be in countless valleys at the same time as He is the great eternal Spirit of God. He can be everywhere, everything and He can do all things.

Section 3

Understanding the Seasons of Life

'To everything there is a season, and a time to every purpose under the heaven: A time to be born, and a time to die; a time to plant, and a time to pluck up that which is planted; A time to kill, and a time to heal; a time to break down, and a time to build up; A time to weep, and a time to laugh; a time to mourn, and a time to dance; A time to cast away stones, and a time to gather stones together; a time to embrace, and a time to refrain from embracing; A time to get, and a time to lose; a time to keep, and a time to cast away; A time to rend, and a time to sew; a time to keep silence, and a time to speak; A time to love, and a time to hate; a time of war, and a time of peace.'

Ecclesiastes 3:1-8

Chapter Seven
A season of loss...

Mum died on 19th April 1997, I had just turned 30. Mum had brought me to live with them as I had lost everything. I was working in Henderson's at the time when she took ill. She was worried about me as I had nowhere to live so was just going from mate to mate, sleeping on sofas so she told me to come back home. Shortly after I had moved into the back room of the house my mum took ill. She was rushed into the Royal hospital and I didn't know if she was dying but knew she was very ill. My brother Stephen and his girlfriend at the time, Michelle were at her bedside as I walked in to visit her.

My mum had seen such a change in me from my previous lifestyle now that I was a Christian. She was sitting upright in the bed with a handkerchief in her hand, her eyes were red from crying. She said to me; "Son, what is it that you have that I don't have? I believe in God but I don't have what you have."

I just said to her; "Mum, I have Jesus in my life." She looked puzzled and asked me what I meant. I said; "The difference is I am not going to church as a religion, I have Jesus in me, I have given my life over completely to him and He lives inside of me."

She said; "Well, how do I get Jesus in my life?"

I said: "You need to get saved."

She said: "Yes, I need saved. I know I need saved." She paused, she played with her handkerchief for a few moments then she looked at me and asked; "How can I be saved?"

I said; "Well, if you know you need saved, call on the name of the Lord and you will be saved." I asked her if she wanted me to pray with her but she said no. She wanted to do it herself. So right there in front of me, Stephen and Michelle, sitting in her hospital bed she bowed her head and gave her life to Christ. She prayed a simple prayer from the heart while she dabbed her eyes with her handkerchief. When she lifted her head, she wiped her eyes and said; "Son, it's done. No more tears."

I went along every single night and read and prayed with her. I remember one night in particular when I arrived, she said; "Son, I am ashamed." I was quite taken aback, I asked her why she was ashamed? She told me that she had woken up the night before in bed and all the things that were going on with her were running around in her head. Because of this she was very afraid and she was ashamed that she was so frightened, she knew she shouldn't have been, because she was saved.

I told her that we all get afraid but when we do, we just need to keep our eyes on the Lord. We can't see *how* things are going to happen, *when* things are going to happen or *how* things will change. I then read to her the passage of Peter getting out of the boat in Matthew 14. After I read it to her, I told her that the Lord called Peter but Peter said; *'Lord, if it be thou, bid me come unto thee on the water.'* The Lord told him to come. Peter stepped out. I said to her; "I am sure Peter was afraid that he was going to sink."

I told her the story, I explained it to her that Peter knew he would sink but when his eyes were on the Lord, he was walking on water. Peter found himself walking on that which others would sink in. That's where your faith comes in, when your eyes are on Christ, you walk on the things you would usually sink in. She said to me; "I see that."

I continued that the winds became boisterous, we are told that the waves came around him. He then put his eyes back on the storm and the sea and he began to sink. Just as I was telling her this story it was really like the word of God was just touching her heart. It illuminated her, her eyes lit up and she said; "I see that, that's what happened to me. I got afraid. I was walking on that sea and I got afraid, son."

I said to her; "Yes, you started thinking about it and your storm got bigger." I asked her what she did when it happened. She said she lay in bed and prayed that the Lord would be with her and help her. She felt calm then and went back to sleep. It soon got to be, that this is all she wanted me to read to her, this became her favourite passage because it was so real to her. So every night I would read this passage and pray with her and she drew strength from the Lord.

Who am I?...

Shortly after, my mum was discharged from hospital and was back home living with me and my dad. I remember one Thursday night I was going out to a meeting, so I said to her that I would be back to see her before she went to sleep. When I came back my dad told me that she was in bed so I just left her, didn't bother disturbing her.

The next day I had a half-day at work so I came home early and my dad said to me: "Your mum was up last night and she was shouting at people who weren't there." I tried to calm him saying that it was just the treatment she was on. I asked him where she was and he said she was in bed. I said I would go up and see her but my dad said; "Before you go up, I am warning you, she won't know who you are."

I said; "Ach, she knows okay. Sure I was talking to her last night and she was fine."

But dad insisted that she wouldn't know, as she didn't know him.

I went on upstairs and opened her door. She was sitting up in the bed watching TV. I walked over and sat beside her and said; "You okay, mum?"

She said; "Aha." That was all she said. I looked over at my dad who was standing at the door and he nodded to go ahead.

I said; "Is everything okay, mum?"

She said; "Yes." I looked at my dad and shrugged my shoulders, he whispered to ask her who I was.

I looked at her and said; "Do you know who I am?"

She looked at me and said; "Of course I do." So again, I looked at my dad as if to say; "What are you talking about?"

I asked her; "Who am I?"

She said; "I don't know."

She never knew me from then on and six weeks later at the age of 53 she passed away in the hospital.

Just before my mum had passed away I had moved in with my older sister Elaine and her daughter Stacy in Ballyduff. Elaine was only two years older than me but a real mummy figure. She looked after me and fed me. The day mum passed away, we were all at the hospital and when the doctor told us that she wasn't getting out, we knew we were losing her. We all sat around her bed just watching her breathing, there were times she struggled with her breathing so they gave her more morphine to help relax her.

She slept away in the early hours of the morning. As she passed away, my brother Stephen was holding her, he had his arm around her body and I was standing beside the bed.

Just as she took her last breath, something happened to me. It was a really strange feeling that passed through me, it was like a surge of power. It took my breath away, I didn't know what it was. I really felt that the Lord was with me, showering me with His peace at the very moment I needed it the most. I don't know what exactly happened to me but I was given great comfort.

I went into the city the next day to register her death and standing at the top of Royal Avenue, I just wanted to shout at everyone to stop! Stop the buses, stop everybody as I wanted them all to know that my mum had died. I wanted to shout it all over the place, I wanted the world to stop but everyone just went on. I was totally devastated.

I buried my mum on the Wednesday and a couple of my friends asked me to go with them to the Cleft in Craigavon on the Saturday night, it was a well-known place for Christian's to hang out. I didn't want to know anybody at that time, or see anyone. My dad encouraged me to go ahead and take myself out, he wanted me to carry on even though he was barely functioning himself. So I did go and that is where I met Alison, just days after burying my precious mum.

Dealing with loss...

Loss is something which comes to all of us at different times and in various stages of hurt. Loss of a job, a home, a car or other personal items can cause a wrench in us that leaves a hurtful disappointment and can be a stressful period in our lives. While the loss to one is great it's almost indifferent to others, yet the loss one suffers however trivial it seems to some others, is still loss. It's their loss, it's personal, it's difficult. This type of loss can be replaced with other things through time but the deep sense of loss that comes from the heart of losing a close loved one is on a completely different level.

Loss may bring a sense of insecurity as that which was firmly in your possession has now gone. Loss can give a sense of failure as that which you deemed in your control has proven to be completely false and so your 'god complex' tells you that it's all your fault and surely you could have done more. Loss lays upon you the sense of guilt and regret with the thought of the *what if's*, the *buts* and the *if only's*.

Loss can bring a range of terrible feelings and every negative impulse that emptiness can throw at you, especially when it's a deep personal loss of a loved one. The cycle of mourning, regretting, wishful thinking, weeping with tears of sadness at every remembrance of the one lost. Good memories make you weep as you want them back again to make some more, while memories which are not so pleasant such as watching loved ones suffer, fight their illness and even take their last breath can cause you to be angry at death. How dare it take away from us our most precious loved ones, or it causes us to feel the unbelief of this terrible nightmare as the finality of it all, triggers a sense of helplessness and injustice.

Loss leaves a vacancy, a void, a great chasm of dread and barrenness deep within which cannot be bound up, neither mollified with ointment. There simply isn't a way to fix it and no earthly medicine for it. "Time is a great healer..." Many may say, but in all reality, it isn't, but time is something that helps you to adjust your life so that you may learn to live differently without those you have lost.

Nostalgia is a blessing and Nostalgia is a curse.

In 1 Samuel 20:18, Jonathan the son of king Saul who was out to slay David, said to David because he was forced to leave... *'thou shalt be missed, because thy seat will be empty.'*

Every time Jonathan would see that seat and David gone, he would have the loss of a great friend come afresh again to him.

A song, a place, an empty chair at dinner, in the living room, every day or at special events and family gatherings throughout the year, or even beside you in church, these everyday situations can cause the wave of grief and the horrifying reality that our loved ones are gone, that their seat is empty.

1 Samuel 20:17 tells us that Jonathan loved David *'as he loved his own soul.'*

That's where true love lies. Deep in the soul. That's where true loss cries. Deep in the soul.

Song of Solomon 8:6 reminds us that 'love is as strong as death.' Death is not the ending of love but those left with that loss do hurt because as strong and as final as death is, so in equal measure is love.

Song of Solomon 8:7; *'Many waters cannot quench love.'*

The waters of time, the waters of Jordan, the waters of separation and the waters of loss, cannot quench love. This reminds me how the love of Christ for us could not be quenched, neither could it be extinguished even though He gave his life on Calvary's tree. In fact I am strengthened and encouraged in the knowledge that He loved us so much that He would allow himself to be taken and crucified to die. His love is as strong as death and not only did his love take him to the cross but it also caused him to rise from the dead, victorious over the grave and because He lives, we shall live also who have placed their trust in Jesus alone. All who die in Christ will also be made alive in Christ and will be together with Christ for eternity.

God has given his word and his promises to us that He would comfort us and bring us through trials and sorrows.

Psalm 71:21; *'Thou shalt increase my greatness, and comfort me on every side.'*

Isaiah 61:1-2; *'The Spirit of the Lord God is upon me; because the Lord hath anointed me to preach good tidings unto the meek; he hath sent me to bind up the brokenhearted, to proclaim liberty to the captives, and the opening of the prison to them that are bound; To proclaim the acceptable year of the Lord, and the day of vengeance of our God; to comfort all that mourn'*

Jesus said in John 14:18; *'I will not leave you comfortless: I will come to you.'*

Comfortless here means orphans. Jesus is promising to come to those who have lost parents. In Psalm 68:5, David says God is *'A father of the fatherless, and a judge of the widows, is God in his holy habitation.'*

The word judge means He will stand up for the widow in her hour of need. He will be her advocate when she has lost her husband, who is her protection.

Isaiah 54:4-5; *'Fear not; for thou shalt not be ashamed: neither be thou confounded; for thou shalt not be put to shame: for thou shalt forget the shame of thy youth, and shalt not remember the reproach of thy widowhood any more. For thy Maker is thine husband; the Lord of hosts is his name; and thy Redeemer the Holy One of Israel; The God of the whole earth shall he be called.'*

We also learn in Proverbs 18:24 that, *'A man that hath friends must shew himself friendly: and there is a friend that sticketh closer than a brother.'*

Loss given to Christ is loss given to love and that love will fill the empty seat in the heart. Remember this. As God, He knows you but as man He understands you. The shortest verse in the Bible is in John 11:35, it simply says; *'Jesus wept.'* He understands your grief, leave your cares with Him and He will comfort you.

Section 4

When two become one

'But from the beginning of the creation God made them male and female. For this cause shall a man leave his father and mother, and cleave to his wife; And they twain shall be one flesh: so then they are no more twain, but one flesh. What therefore God hath joined together, let not man put asunder.'

Mark 10:6-9

Chapter Eight
Meeting Alison...

We drove up to the Craigavon Civic Centre that Saturday night and arrived at the Cleft. There was a big crowd, it was organised by a man called Clive Elliott. He asked where we were from, so he shouted at the girls serving the tea to make us feel welcome. Alison was one of the girls serving the tea and that was how we met, the first time I saw her she poured me a cup of tea, little did I know, she would be pouring me tea all these years later!

Two weeks later, we went to the Cleft again and I got chatting with Alison afterwards. We invited her and her friend to come to church. So, the next morning they arrived at Whitewell to see us. At this time I was house sitting a Baptist preacher's home as I had nowhere to live. So after church, they came to the house and we had tea and it was when we were sitting chatting that I realised that Alison was only 19 and I was 30 so I thought it was never going to work. Then to make it worse, I also found out that she was from the other end of the world – a small village way, way, way from Belfast called Donaghcloney.

To me the world was flat and dropped off at Finaghy on the Belfast boundary so I had no idea where Donaghcloney was, it was just going to be too far away for me. My mate took a shine to Alison's friend so as they spent time together, me and Alison got chatting more and more. He then asked her out and while doing so told Alison that I fancied her but I hadn't said anything of the sort, to me she was too young and too far away. He then told me that

Alison wanted me to ask her out but neither of us had said these things. The both of us were being set up!

We were sitting one Saturday night chatting in the house I was looking after and I thought, well I might as well try so I, being the slick guy that I am just casually slipped my arm around her and she moved away. Then I realised I had been set up. I was fed up so I said to them that I was going for a Chinese and the next thing, Alison was jumping to her feet saying that she was going too. I thought; "Hold on a minute, after you rejecting me?" So we went to the Chinese and when we were coming back in through the door, are you ready for this?... Alison jumped me and gave me a big kiss on the doorstep!

ALISON: I got saved on the 14th March, shortly after this I went to a Free Presbyterian youth rally and the preacher said that we shouldn't run around dating but we should pray and ask God for a husband so I thought that was exactly what I would do, I would pray about it and ask God. I often joke that you should be careful what you pray for as I had then met Ken a month later! When I got saved, I was with my friend and her sister, we all met the Lord together. My friend was very outgoing and had wanted to get us involved in things so we went along to the Cleft and were only there one night and she had us signed up to help at it.

That night, I was told to serve tea to the guys from Belfast and that was when I first saw Ken. My first impression of Ken was that he looked pretty rough and tough, he had a shaved head but something that I noticed more than anything was his blue eyes. He had really bright blue eyes which caught my attention and I remember thinking; "He's not bad." But nonetheless I was still praying for my husband, not realising that Ken was him.

When we saw each other two weeks later at the Cleft, afterwards we sat chatting in my car and I remember at the time, it was like no one else was in the car. Our friends were sitting chatting in the back but I was completely oblivious to them. Ken and I had so much to talk about.

I remember the night we were all watching a movie at Ken's house and he just slipped his arm around me, I thought he was a bit forward so I moved away.

However, when he said he was going to get the Chinese, I was in. The way to my heart was food. Now on our return I was standing at the door holding the Chinese, looking up at Ken and waiting for him to open the door when he kissed me! It wasn't the other way around!

After a couple of weeks I knew Ken was the man for me. I knew he was concerned about the age gap and the physical distance between us but as far as I was concerned - he was the one. I knew my parents wouldn't approve of the age gap, so I devised a plan. I spoke to my mum's friend Barbara, who was like an aunt to me and confided in her about Ken, she agreed with me that my mum and dad wouldn't be happy. Together we decided to take mum out for the day, we drove to Portrush, took her around the coast and bought lunch. I had primed Barbara that over lunch when I told mum about the age gap that she would calm her down by saying; "Age is only a number."

As planned, I told mum that Ken was a lovely fella, we were getting on great but there was only one problem, that he was ten years older. (I decided ten sounded better.) I could see mum going; "What?" Then Barbara cut in; "Och sure, age is only a number."

And before we knew it, mum was agreeing, that yes, that was true. She said; "If he is the one then I suppose it doesn't matter." I was telling her that it was of the Lord, trying to convince her. Like, how could you argue with the Lord?

She agreed to meet Ken but she did warn me that Dad wouldn't be putting out the welcome mat for him as she knew he would not approve. My Dad was a prison officer in the famous HMP Maze, that housed Loyalist and Republican prisoners in the H-Blocks. For him to meet an older man with a shaved head from the Shore Road after his daughter, well we knew he would not be offering Ken 'high tea.'

My mum is a great mother but she has a weakness, she's not the best at keeping a secret. I had told her in confidence, as a mother-daughter moment that I really felt Ken was going to be my husband. I told her that I knew it was very early, we hadn't even started dating but I confided in her my feelings. I felt very strongly that Ken was the man I had been praying for, he was the husband that I was going to have. So days later and the first time my mum meets Ken, much to my embarrassment, she says to him; "My daughter believes she is going to marry you!"

I went and picked Alison up, to go out for the day, it was the first time I had been at her house. When I arrived, I was brought into the kitchen and I was so taken aback by the house, compared to where I was from - it was something else! This massive bungalow set on its own land, I felt really intimidated by it all. To me it was like something out of the Dallas TV series. It was pure luxury.

Their kitchen was the size of the whole house I grew up in and it just displayed grandeur. As Alison was getting ready, her mum greeted me and if only I had a warning how tactful her mum was – not!

I was standing next to the sink and noticed the window was open. I have to admit I was wondering if I could fit through the window when her mum addressed me with her first words; "I don't know what your intentions are with my daughter?" I looked at the window again!!

She continued; "Alison tells me you are the man she is going to marry." She just stared at me, I stuttered; "Did she? What?" I was so shocked.

Eunice said; "Yes, she did." I was speechless, my mouth went dry and I could feel sweat appearing, all hitting me at once... HELP! And this was only our first date.

Alison appeared and off we went to Murlough Bay. As I was thinking the whole thing through, my conclusion was, I didn't think it was going to work. To me, we were worlds apart in every way. I tried to take it in my stride and we carried on with our picnic, all was okay until I mentioned the conversation to Alison and she nearly died! She was mortified that her mum had said that to me.

Meeting Ken...

I had become a Christian on that Friday night and the following Sunday I was taken to Whitewell Tabernacle in Belfast. I walked into Whitewell expecting it to be the same as the Brethren or Free Presbyterian churches I was used to but this was so different. I had never saw people standing worshipping God before and the singing was great with the large choir leading in every song. They sang the song *'He is always there for me'* which wasn't a traditional hymn that I knew but hearing that chorus that day really meant something to me. Even as I write my part in this book, I will always remember that Pastor McConnell's ministry taught me how to love the Lord. Even hearing those words, coming from my traditional background was a little weird as nobody would ever have said that they loved the Lord. That wasn't the word people used, it wasn't a language people used. I was used to hearing about repenting or going to hell but love? Love wasn't talked about and being in a love relationship with the Lord was completely different again.

So that was my first Sunday experience and from then on I had a real hunger to know everything I could about the Lord and enter a love relationship with Him. I would have went to meetings all over the country, as I just wanted to learn more, to know more about Him. Even to the point of going to church three times in the one day! How things had changed for me.

As I always loved going out on a Saturday night, I did wonder what Christians were supposed to do on this night. So we discovered The Cleft in Craigavon. It was a large gathering of young people on a Saturday night. We met the organiser Clive and he probably felt we were like a whirlwind coming in, he was very taken with our stories and asked us to testify. He was also setting up a welcoming committee and asked us to be part of it. So, only saved for a couple of weeks, here I was at this large meeting testifying to everyone. I was at last enjoying life and feeling the satisfaction and fullness that had been missing for so long.

I could have went out with men but the problem I had was I always got bored with them. I loved the chase and the idea of them but the reality was often a let-down. Sometimes you have to kiss a few frogs until you find your prince! That's probably what blew Mum's mind as I told her I had met someone I thought I was going to marry. That is very foreign talk for her daughter. I don't know how I knew that about Ken, other than the Lord revealed it to me.

I knew my feelings for Ken were completely different than anything I had experienced before. I missed him if I didn't see him or talk to him. I felt part of me was missing when I wasn't with him.

He made me laugh, I had fallen in love with him. Though I would say my biggest attraction to Ken was not just his baby-blue eyes but the fact that he loved the Lord and wanted to serve Him.

When I met Ken I just knew that we would marry and I am a really practical person so I thought to myself; "If this is the man I am going to marry, he is a few years older than me so we don't have a whole pile of time to waste." So I wasn't interested in waiting for years and trailing out a long engagement, I thought we should just get married. Ken likes to tell people that I just couldn't keep my hands off him but I just didn't see the logic in delaying the inevitable.

I remember my granny told me; "Alison, just make sure of one thing. Make sure he is more spiritual than you. If he has a stronger relationship with the Lord, he will encourage you and lift you up rather than drag you down." Now reader, that is good advice.

I was looking for someone who loved the Lord more than me and I saw that in Ken. The Scriptures tell us; *'Her sins, which are many, are forgiven; for she loved much: but to whom little is forgiven, the same loveth little.'* Luke 7:47. Ken had been forgiven so much that he loved the Lord so much. There was nothing he wouldn't do so before we were even married, Ken was working in the church, doing anything that he could do to serve the Lord. I just enjoyed helping Ken in whatever he was doing. If he was distributing tracts, I went with him and helped. I was always at his side, no matter what it was or where it was.

I knew within myself that Ken was going to do something for the Lord. At that time he was working in Henderson's but I knew he was going to serve the Lord. The practical side of me was thinking, if Ken was going to be a pastor then he needed a wife. He didn't need a long drawn out relationship but he needed his personal life grounded. He had a work to do so I thought it was something we could do together.

Ken really swept me off my feet. We were quite an intense

couple, it was a whirlwind romance. When I met Ken he was heartbroken about his mum and I think in a lot of ways, I would say I became more of a replacement, nurturer or carer as I would do practical things for him. Cook for him or buy him dinners and leave him in an extra one. Get him groceries to make sure he would have something to eat. Even now, twenty years later if I am out and Ken is studying, he forgets to eat so I would always leave him something. He is spoilt! I'd sort his washing and ironing, but mainly I was an ear that he could talk to about his mum and his grief and how he was feeling.

Chapter Nine
Dating...

When we were first dating, Ken invited me down to his house for dinner. I was really excited as I thought; "Happy days, I have found a man that can cook." As all the cooking in my house was done by mum, I didn't have any ideas about how to make meals. So I went down and he had the table set lovely. He brought me in a nice glass of *Shloer*, it was all looking very promising. Then he went to get the dinner, well my mouth nearly hit the ground. He gave me a plate of Smash and beans! Smash? I am a country girl, used to real potatoes. I was disgusted! Suddenly my rose-tinted glasses were 'smashed!'

To add insult to injury, the next time I went to Ken's house for dinner, he did the same again! Only this time it was Smash and peas! He was really inspirational.

The first time I was gracious and ate it but this time I wasn't having it. I just told him that I couldn't eat it, it's not even real potato! And with peas? He didn't even put meat with it? So I told him to forget it - my treat, we were having Chinese. That was the end of Ken's cooking career.

Taking the next step...

I knew Alison was the one for me so I decided it was time to take the next step. I spoke to her mum about proposing but she told me I really needed to speak to her dad, Stan. I was shocked to hear that and was a little put off as her dad and I hadn't really hit it off. I knew he was wary of me but I had no choice.

I walked into the living room, he was sitting on his chair by the fire. I could feel my heart thumping out of my chest. I walked straight over to him and said; "Stan, is it okay if I marry your daughter?" I could feel the sweat break on me.

He just looked at me and jokingly said; "Aye, take her out of my road."

I couldn't believe it! I said; "Okay thanks." And that was it. We didn't speak of it again.

Alison and I then went and looked at rings. To be honest, I just couldn't afford one. I had no idea how expensive they were. At that time I was still paying off debt and things were extremely tight. I just couldn't understand how they could cost so much!

ALISON: I was so excited, Ken had taken me to a jewellers in Belfast to look at rings. We looked at the window display, my eyes lit up, they were beautiful. It was fashionable then for everyone to have gold rings but I didn't like gold, I wanted something different. I liked silver jewellery. We went in and I enquired about an alternative to gold. The sales assistant produced a platinum ring and poor Ken nearly had heart failure! He was looking at the prices but I wasn't interested in what they cost, I just wanted to find the right one for me. I tried on a few then I spotted one that was a mix of gold and silver and I just loved it. It was gorgeous! I thought it was a practical ring as with it having the two colours mixed, then I would never be tied in the future if my taste changed. I knew it was the one but when I looked at the price tag, it was me who nearly fainted as I knew Ken could never afford it. It was £1,500 which was a LOT of money back then, especially to us. It was devastating, as it was beautiful.

I knew as soon as Alison saw that ring, there was no option, she had to have it. I thought I was going to pass out at the price! I told her it was just way out of my price range and she pretended to be okay with that but I knew her heart was set. I didn't want to disappoint her so I went back to the jewellers on my own and spoke to the lady who had helped us. She agreed that I could pay it off. Now, I had no idea how I was going to do that and with Alison wanting to be engaged asap – the pressure was on. So I started working all hours, taking on extra jobs, labouring, just whatever I could do to raise the money. I am not even sure how I did it but within a few months, the ring was paid. Now I just had to pop the question!

I arranged to take Alison out one day, I knew she wasn't feeling the best but I didn't care, I had lost blood, sweat and tears getting this ring so I wanted it on her finger! I insisted we go for a drive, I took her to the North Down coast. There was a yacht club along the coast road which I thought would be a nice place to propose.

We drove down into the park facing the yacht club and I thought I would get Alison out of the car for a walk. It was getting a little dark and the lights from the club were reflecting on the water, it was a romantic scene.

I got out of the car and walked around to her door and opened it but Alison didn't want to get out. She was loaded with the cold and wanted to stay in the car. It was slowly turning into a disaster, I didn't know what to do. As I stood there beside the car of course the heavens opened and it poured! So I was standing in the rain and Alison is sitting in the car feeling really miserable. I thought that there was nothing else for it, so I got down on my knee in the rain and I said; "Will you marry me?"

And she said; "No!"

I said; "No?"

And then she said; "I mean yes!"

I said to her; "Make up your mind!"

I produced the ring and Alison miraculously healed! All of a sudden all her cold symptoms disappeared, she wanted to go and show off her new ring to all her friends.

Learning to prioritise...

I had got myself a small one-bedroom flat in Mount Vernon, it was a famous part of Belfast but not for good reasons. The block of flats housed paramilitaries, prostitutes etc. but I talked to them all, inviting them into my house, witnessing to them day and night. Then we would regularly put tracts in through all the doors on the estate and we started a Saturday club to help the young people.

We were very busy, every night of the week we were out serving the Lord. Life was busy but it became clear that if we were going to get married then we should really spend some time together, we were always with others but not alone, not having quality time.

ALISON: I suggested to Ken that he could give up the Friday night scouts so we could spend more time together. On a Friday night, Ken drove the scouts to the centre and waited outside for an hour and a half and then drove them back. I thought this was a waste of time and would be a good night to drop so we could have some quality time together. When I said to him about it, his response was... "If you think you are going to take me away from the Lord and His work - you can just go now!"

I was gobsmacked, I was only asking for one night and he was getting rid of me! Ken called the engagement off, I was so shocked, I thought it was a complete overreaction. I left the flat and got into my car and just couldn't take in what had just happened. I wasn't going to let it go, I went over to the intercom system and buzzed Ken. When he answered I asked him if he was serious? He told me to come back upstairs so we sat down and talked it through and sorted it out.

I sat and listened to Alison's request again and realised that a compromise had to be made and that compromise must be made by me. Alison went with me and she backed me in everything. Surely one night out of seven wouldn't hurt. I wasn't even in the scouts but had just been asked to help them on a temporary basis. I had felt to not drive that bus would be me letting the Lord down from my promise to serve Him with all that I am and have. I wrestled with the thought of this, of whether this was conviction to keep my word or a trial of faith to keep going or was it condemnation from the Lord to keep me working for Him? The penny suddenly dropped! It was none of these things!

I realised that the Lord Jesus who loved me while I was in my sinful lifestyle and an enemy of His, who died for me, who saved me, rescued me and delivered me, was this same Jesus, who loved me eternally.

He loved me in spite of me and not because of me. And no matter the amount of service, whether more or less, it couldn't cause Him to love me any less nor would He forsake me.

As it says in Romans 5:6-8; *'For when we were yet without strength, in due time Christ died for the ungodly. For scarcely for a righteous man will one die: yet peradventure for a good man some would even dare to die. But God commendeth his love toward us, in that, while we were yet sinners, Christ died for us.'*

We must also believe the promise in Hebrews 13:5; *'for he hath said, I will never leave thee, nor forsake thee.'*

We must be careful in our walk with God, to always remember that falling from grace is not necessarily failing to go on with God and going into the world. Falling from grace is also going on with God in labour and not in love. It's doing the work of the Lord and forgetting the Lord of the work. *'Faith without works is dead.'* (James 2:26)

And we also know James 2:18; *'Yea, a man may say, Thou hast faith, and I have works: shew me thy faith without thy works, and I will shew thee my faith by my works.'*

Yet at the cost of grace, many tend to labour until they burn out or they work until they blow out or blow up!

Philippians 1:22; *'But if I live in the flesh, this is the fruit of my labour: yet what I shall choose I wot not.'*

Alison was not a condemnation nor a test from the Lord. She was a voice of reason to an enthusiastic young man who was on the road to burnout. After all, God rested on the seventh day and Jesus said in Mark 6:31; *'Come ye yourselves apart into a desert place, and rest a while'*… Or as someone once said; "Come apart before you come apart!"

I agreed with her – she was right. God would not condemn me for taking one night off, as it says in Romans 8:1; *'There is therefore now no condemnation to them which are in Christ Jesus, who walk not after the flesh, but after the Spirit.'*

I was well-meaning and sincere but I was starting to trust in me and my works and I realised the flesh is really subtle and I was working more and more in the flesh. The flesh of righteousness works, of keeping myself rather than resting in grace! I grasped hold of 1Peter 1:5; *'Who are kept by the power of God through faith unto salvation ready to be revealed in the last time.'*

This would also be a stumbling block for marriage and ministry, although it took me sometime to grasp the truth and the essential necessity of it.

The order is, Christ first, your wife next and then the church/ministry. Ephesians 5:25 tells us; *'Husbands, love your wives, even as Christ also loved the church, and gave himself for it.'* Now that's a tall order! Christ died for us! Before we become a husband, consider Christ as you also have to lay down your life for her!

So I went and gave a month's notice and took the Friday evenings off.

The wedding...

With Ken's mum only recently dying and his dad not being too well, we decided to keep the wedding low-key. Unfortunately due to his poor health, Ken's dad wasn't able to attend. My father had given us an option of either having a big wedding and blowing the budget or we could have a smaller wedding and use the rest of the money to buy a car. As we desperately needed a car at that time, we decided to keep it small. It was an intimate wedding, just immediate family and we didn't have an after-party.

I will never forget arriving up to the doors in Whitewell to be told by one of the guests that the groom, best man and ushers were missing! It was quite a shock! It turned out that they were playing snooker in the youth hall! I had to do a lap of the Shore Road until they got them into the church.

We were married in the Magee room in Whitewell. It's a beautiful library, we had fifty guests consisting of family and close friends. Then we had a wedding reception in the Tullymore House in Broughshane.

At our reception instead of Ken giving a speech, he preached his first sermon on the text *'lovest thou me more than these?'* (John 21:15) He spoke on loving the Lord more than the world.

The next day we flew out from Dublin for our honeymoon in Gran Canaria.

Two becoming one under God...

Genesis 2:24; *'Therefore shall a man leave his father and his mother, and shall cleave unto his wife: and they shall be one flesh.'*

This is rehearsed in Ephesians 5:31, where the Apostle Paul likens a husband and his wife as one in unity, in the same sense that Christ and his church are one. The unity and the intimacy of the couple should be held as precious, personal and sanctified, as it's a type of the body of Christ. One spirit, one life, one body, one goal, one vision, one mind.

Love for one another is the draw to intimacy, while intimacy is the key to unity and unity enables the flow of blessing, whether it's within the confines of a marriage and a home, or in the service of Christ. Two become one under God with the intimacy and unity of that oneness bearing fruit in the natural and the spiritual realm, in children, family, increasing joy, growth and ability in helping and blessing others.

Ephesians 5 leaves a tall order for both husband and wife featuring love and respect. Oh how we do falter and have miserably failed many times. As it says in verses 24-25; *'Therefore as the church is subject unto Christ, so let the wives be to their own husbands in every thing. Husbands, love your wives, even as Christ also loved the church, and gave himself for it.'*

Christ is the one and only head of the church and wives are likened to the church under their husband in order to be one body and of one accord.

This can be difficult, especially in this modern era. Some women are abused and treated terribly by their husbands and so we must ask; is this acceptable then? We must answer with an emphatic reply; God forbid! Absolutely not!

This passage also gives every husband a tall order; *'Husbands, love your wives, even as Christ also loved the church, and gave himself for it.'*

The husband's tall order from God's word, is to love our wives but more than that, it's to love her as much as Christ loved you, brother, and gave his life for you.

Now if husband's can do that, then surely their wives would be secure to know that they are in safe hands and under the protection of a godly man, worthy of respect and love in return with the pattern being as said in 1 John 4:19; *'We love him, because he first loved us.'*

Ephesians 5:32; *'This is a great mystery: but I speak concerning Christ and the church.'* If there's a breakdown of love and respect in the church or lack of love and intimacy between the church and Christ then blessing stops and strain starts to show. Yet, Christ loves his own and so the breakdown never comes from Him as He is always the same and it's the church who fails him.

1 Corinthians 13:4-8; *'Charity suffereth long, and is kind; charity envieth not; charity vaunteth not itself, is not puffed up, Doth not behave itself unseemly, seeketh not her own, is not easily provoked, thinketh no evil; Rejoiceth not in iniquity, but rejoiceth in the truth; Beareth all things, believeth all things, hopeth all things, endureth all things. Charity never faileth: but whether there be prophecies, they shall fail; whether there be tongues, they shall cease; whether there be knowledge, it shall vanish away.'*

The Lord Jesus loves his church as his own body, as it says in Ephesians 5:30; *'For we are members of his body, of his flesh, and of his bones.'*

Being in Christ we do not have a choice, because He loved us, we must love each other!

Section 5

Hard times can be God's tool to refine us...

'Wherein ye greatly rejoice, though now for a season, if need be, ye are in heaviness through manifold temptations: That the trial of your faith, being much more precious than of gold that perisheth, though it be tried with fire, might be found unto praise and honour and glory at the appearing of Jesus Christ.'

1 Peter 1:6-7

Chapter Ten
Jekyll and Hyde?...

The first year of marriage was the roughest and one of the toughest years I ever had. The man I knew before we got married was very romantic and thoughtful and after we married I started to think, who did I marry, a Dr Jekyll and Mr Hyde? All the romance seemed to disappear overnight.

There was tremendous stress on our relationship after we married. I think it was difficult as we were clearly two very different people and to be honest, we didn't really know each other at all.

On paper, Ken and I as a married couple shouldn't work. There were so many differences yet the love we had for each other seemed to overcome all of the challenges. There are eleven years between us, yet most of the time I feel I am the older, more sensible one!

And after twenty years of marriage I never even think of the age difference. Should a problem arise in my marriage, the first thing I do is get in contact with my counsellor. In my first years of marriage, I spent a lot of time on my knees talking to Christ, my counsellor. His name shall be called Wonderful, Counsellor, Almighty God, the Prince of Peace.

After spending time in prayer, I realised I was not perfect and neither was my husband. It was on one such occasion when the Lord gave me advice on how to handle my husband's temper, yes, he had a temper! Proverbs 15:1 tells us; *A soft answer turneth away wrath: but grievous words stir up anger.* I learned that instead of being a sparring partner, I was to have wisdom and a soft answer.

Instead of just telling your partner you love them, I have always found showing it instead of saying it was the best proof of the love. Love is an action. You show your love by all the little things you do for each other. Romans 5:8; *'God commandeth His love toward us, in that while we were yet sinners, Christ died for us.'*

When we were in our sin and unlovable – Love died for us in the person of Christ.

KEN: Marriage and getting used to living together can be a little stressful to say the least. There's the different likes and dislikes, there's the sleeping habits, the stress of work, cleaning, household duties, cooking and of course paying the bills. It's all too easy for a couple to give up and walk away at the first sign of hardship but it must be remembered that although the person seems different, so might you be!

It must also be brought to mind that sometimes couples can get an unrealistic view of their spouse. Expect too much and you will always be disappointed. Though all manner of physical, emotional, mental and sexual abuse must never be deemed acceptable, yet in a marriage, one can expect stress and a little character change. Finally, if a person changes one way then they can certainly change another. If they both stay in love with Jesus, then they can stay in love with each other. Take everything to the Lord in prayer, both together and in your individual devotional time.

One might say; "It's not a great compromise to give up one night driving a bus for a group that you weren't even in!" And they may be right, but the point is, sometimes we get into a mindset and our motive becomes a misguided mission.

The object wasn't the size or the greatness of the compromise but rather the actual yielding to what God wanted for me and from me.

To surrender to His will, brings supply from His hands. A heart fully at peace is the result of a will fully yielded to the will of God.

Remember this; if you can't be faithful in the small things, you won't be faithful in the bigger things.

God was preparing me to serve my wife.

A dangerous journey...

I moved into the flat with Ken, it gave me a great prayer life as every time I used the lift, I prayed that nobody would join me! The surrounding flats were full of drunkards, paramilitaries, prostitutes etc. so I was praying hard that I would be okay. I was always praying; "Please Lord, don't let anyone get into this lift." But then I would enter our 'apartment' and they would all be in there anyway, so what was the point?

At that time Ken was not working due to an accident he had at work, so he would be spending his time telling everybody about God. I was the breadwinner at that time, working in a nursery in Banbridge then driving up and down every day from Belfast.

I remember one-night driving home from Banbridge and I knew I had been really tired and I was wore out, but instead of being really practical and slowing down, I continued on as needs must, I needed to work. But as I was driving along the Westlink, coming into Belfast, my body shut down. Just as it used to do. I knew instantly that I was going to pass out.

I panicked - what was I going to do? I told the Lord; "Lord, you need to get me home!" I put the car windows down to try and get some air around me, I switched on the radio to try and keep focused. Somehow or other, I got back to the flat and was so exhausted and drained I could not get out of the car.

Ken had looked out and saw me pull in so he came downstairs wondering why I wasn't moving. He had to help me out of the car and up to the flat. He was really worried, he asked me what was wrong? I knew what it was, I knew the feeling only too well. The M.E. had returned.

From a husband to a carer...

I had never experienced anything like what I saw happening to Alison. When she left in the morning she was great, yes a little tired but in good form. We had been talking about what we were doing later that evening, making plans for the weekend but when she arrived home from work... it was like something from *Invasion of the Body Snatchers*. Was she really there at all?

She had no strength, she couldn't walk. I had to lift her out of the car and more or less trail her up to the flat. I lay her down and she seemed to pass in and out of consciousness. It was really disturbing. I just couldn't get it, I couldn't understand what was going on before my eyes. It was surreal. I knew something was really wrong. I told her to lie down and rest but I was worried, deeply worried.

As the days passed, Alison had no strength and I couldn't understand what was wrong with her, I was always on the go and just couldn't get why she was lying about constantly. Part of me just wanted to give her a shake. She was younger than me but I was the one with all the energy - it just didn't make sense.

Alison was sleeping all day, she would have got up to eat something in the evening but then she went back to bed. We weren't married long at this stage and suddenly my wife had disappeared and if anything, I was her carer rather than her husband.

She slept all the time but she always made an effort to go to the Lord's table on a Sunday morning. I took her home afterwards and she went straight back to bed, sometimes having enough strength for the evening service, other times she just couldn't go but she never missed communion.

It was a huge effort for her to go to church and it was embarrassing for her too as Whitewell was such a large church and quite often she would just collapse and that was her away. I had to carry her out of church many times. It was like a fear swept across her face, I could see it coming, her body tightened and within seconds she was gone. She was like a life-size rag doll. Her body just went limp and she went into shut-down mode.

Some of the other pastors would have helped me carry her to the car. Suddenly M.E. became very real to me. Before this, when I had heard about it, I thought it was like having the flu, but far from it. I often watched Alison, especially in church just start to sweat. Really sweat, the beads running down her face and it was that look she gave me, it was like she was saying 'oh no' and I knew she was scared. We were stuck between a rock and a hard place, we were asking; "Why, God?" We were praying for healing but seeing no breakthrough.

I will always remember one Sunday morning we were in the flat getting ready to go to church and Alison was wearing a long pale blue dress, I spoke into the bedroom to her asking if she was nearly ready, she said she was. I went into the kitchen to lift a few things and a couple of minutes later I went back to check on her and she was standing staring at me and her blue dress had changed colour, it was really dark. Just absolutely saturated in sweat and I just went 'oh no' and leapt across the room to where she was standing and just got her in time before she collapsed. It was days like that I realised this was no flu, this was a real illness and my wife was suffering badly.

Our lives had changed dramatically, suddenly I was doing the shopping and cleaning and our relationship became strained. I was washing Alison and at times had to feed her too. It was a far cry from the life we had envisaged having together. I had heard stories about how M.E. had affected Alison as a young girl but the reality was much worse. She had been a highly energised woman but now it literally was like someone had pulled the plug out with her, she just shut down within seconds and she was out.

With Alison being so ill, we decided to leave the flat as it wasn't helping the situation. It was so tiny. We moved to Deacon Street, near Tiger's Bay, with the help of Alison's parents, we purchased a four-bedroom house to give us more space. We were happier there.

We weren't in Deacon Street long and Alison took another 'nosedive' with her symptoms getting worse. I remember her just sitting there on the settee staring blankly ahead. I sprinkled some sugar on cornflakes, thinking it might give her a boost. I fed them to her, most of them dripping out of her mouth but I tried my best. I just looked at the bowl to get another spoonful and when I turned back to her - she was away, slumped down on the chair beside me.

At the time I felt really hindered in my work for the Lord, but looking back now I see that my ministry at that time was to care for my wife. I wanted to be out doing, not stuck at home. Back then I thought the Lord's work was out knocking doors, doing children's work etc. but my first port of call in the Lord's work should have been my wife. In hindsight and wisdom now looking back, I know I should have done more for Alison.

The night I got saved, I told the Lord that I had nothing to give Him, my body was wrecked. I know salvation is free, it is only by grace, but I told Him that I had nothing to give, all I had was myself. I sold myself totally out to him, I gave Him my life - my whole life. So this season with Alison being ill was hard as I wasn't able to be out doing what I thought was the Lord's work. Little did I know then that the Lord was using this time to knit us together and make us stronger for the days ahead.

I got myself so hung up on the fact that I wasn't being true to God, I gave Him my word and now I wasn't keeping it. If Alison was sleeping, I knew that she would be okay for a few hours so I would go out and do what I could. We didn't have mobile phones back then so I couldn't check on her remotely, and so had to just trust she would be okay. I just was so torn in my life, it was a difficult season for me to grasp all that was taking place.

ALISON: It was a difficult season for both of us, I had such an overwhelming feeling at that time that I was letting Ken down as I wasn't fulfilling my wifely duties. I was the 'younger model' as such and I was no use to him, I was holding him back from his ministry. I couldn't do anything for myself, my body was so weak. Ken was doing the housework, the cooking and just everything. It was awful.

We were still only married a short time and now he was my full-time carer. I also knew that Ken was embarrassed when I conked out in public, he was the one that was left to carry my lifeless body out of church. My mood was very low at this point, it was hard to see God's plan for my life.

It was a hard time in our marriage as Ken was still trying to be as involved in church as much as possible, running constantly to meetings and leaving me behind. I remember different times just thinking, 'are you really going out and leaving me again?' but away he went.

I remember one time him coming home with a bunch of flowers, he wasn't home till about 1am. I knew he was at a meeting but I felt so hurt that he had left me for all of that time and it didn't cost him a thought. Ken just didn't understand how his actions were hurting me and I didn't tell him as I didn't see the point, I just knew he wouldn't get it.

A lot of people didn't understand my illness, I was

quite often told to... "Just shake it off..." I learned to smile graciously at them but inside I was screaming; "I would if I could, you idiot!" There is such a lack of understanding around invisible illnesses, it really makes it harder.

Also, I found my own mentality factored a lot as with me taking M.E. at fourteen, it effected me physically. I missed out on sports at school and when I recovered, I still felt very much that my body was limited.

My mentality then was very much that I didn't know if I was able to do something active, if I did then I would be risking something. I accepted that I was limited by my body so I chose to miss out on most physical activities just in case. I didn't know if I went jogging, how far I would get or if I would pay a physical price for doing it, so I just didn't try it. I kept living within the limits of M.E. even when I knew I was recovering and was doing really well.

Chapter Eleven
Ministry-focused or God-focused?

Our marriage was going through a turbulent time, the more Ken told me to 'shake myself,' the more I wanted to shake him! There were certainly a lot of days I just cried to God as I didn't think this was going to work out at all. We were so different and Ken just didn't understand what I was going through, he certainly didn't realise the extent that I just wanted him to be with me, he was ministry-focused instead of God-focused. What's the difference? God is family first, ministry second, it's only when we have these in the right order that unison will be in the family. The more I tried to have him at home with me, the more he pulled away and the more the 'Davidson temper' was really starting to feature heavily in our marriage.

For me personally, I wasn't able to fulfil all my marital duties as I wasn't well. It just couldn't happen and I was just no use to him. Even just the basic things of looking after him, cleaning or cooking for him. All of these things were on hold, I just couldn't do them. This affected me on top of my illness as I just didn't feel good about myself in any way.

Ken had so much going on when I first met him that he came to me with a lot of baggage. With the loss of his mummy, he was grieving. He was up and down and was very quick-tempered. Our marriage was a real challenge, it certainly wasn't the one I had considered having. They say that love blinds and boy was I blind in love! I had just turned 20 and I had this idea that the guy who swept me off my feet was the guy I was going to be married to. The Ken I dated was not the Ken I was married to. Obviously when I took ill, romance went clean out the window. Even if you were like us with no money, it would have meant the world to me if Ken had of just brought home some wild flowers for me, or a bar of chocolate and gave me the last piece. Now you might be thinking, it's all about me. No, it's not! Scripture says, '*Husbands, love your wives, even as Christ also loved the church, and gave himself for it.*' Ephesians 5:25.

Can you see, Christ GAVE Himself for it. Jesus was not putting Himself first, He was putting you and me first, sacrificing the glory (what He had) to what He was willing to further give. Likewise, when a man decides to marry, in Christ he will put you before his desires. Let's see how this man of God whom I love unfolds into a husband of Christ.

With no furniture, other than Ken's sister, Elaine's, spare room couch and a lack of finances, this created a powder keg called Ken. Obviously, you try and learn how to live with your husband, you figure him out as he in turn is figuring you out. Now I know what he is thinking, I could read his mind but back then, communication was terrible! He didn't connect with me, his idea of communicating was normally when he got angry. If he was cross then I figured he had something to say but then because he was angry, I shut down.

I wasn't going to listen to him when he was like that. He bottled up his feelings and especially about his mum, he didn't deal with the grief. It was two years after her death before he actually broke down about it. He would have talked to me about his mum but always as a third person, like he was detached from the situation. I was always concerned that he hadn't taken the time to grieve and that caused major problems. My illness certainly put a lot of pressure on our marriage as we were both frustrated. I was frustrated because I wasn't able to be the wife I wanted to be. Ken was frustrated as he was praying continually for me and nothing was changing. It was a hard season, as I remember him praying faithfully, reminding me of the Scripture; *'Ask, and it shall be given you; seek, and ye shall find; knock, and it shall be opened unto you: For every one that asketh receiveth; and he that seeketh findeth; and to him that knocketh it shall be opened.'* Matthew 7:7-8.

Then I could have had maybe two or even three really good days but then I was at rock bottom again, this was very discouraging for us. He went back to what he knew best and threw himself into the ministry, he was serving in the church every day. I think he was just busying himself as he felt he was no use to me but resentment started to rise in me as he wasn't there when I really needed him the most. My mum had to look after me as Ken was out day and night, ministry was again coming first. With no quality time together, things started to fall apart. Instead of Ken caring for me, I was reliant on my mum. Everything was against us. It was only the Lord that got us through.

One day I was sitting alone, as per usual in the house and the Lord showed me a Scripture, it said; *'A soft answer turneth away wrath.'* Proverbs 15:1. When I read that I understood it completely, I knew it was for our situation. At that point, Ken was still reacting to his mum just having passed away and I knew a lot of that anger was being directed at me. Most people at some point will take their anger out on those who are nearest to them until they realise, anger will sow seeds of discord in a relationship.

When Ken came in that afternoon, he was giving off as per usual but I sat my ground, I decided I wasn't going to argue with him. When I didn't rise to what Ken wanted, it made him worse, now he was really cross! So he yelled at me; "Right that's it, I have had enough of this marriage!" He slammed the door and walked out. I remember just sitting on the chair and exhaling deeply - it was a relief. I didn't cry which would have been expected, but instead I just felt relieved. I was quite happy that he had called time on the marriage, it obviously just wasn't meant to be after all.

After a while, Ken came back and said sorry to me, so I was

just honest with him, I told him instead of sitting feeling broken-hearted, which I should have been, I explained that I felt relieved because I just couldn't live like that. I was brought up in a Christian home with no arguments or fighting, if you needed to deal with something then you sat down and talked it out. I wasn't used to this environment at all and I didn't want to get used to it. When I said this to Ken, it really shocked him. Telling him that was one of the best things I could have done, as from that night on our marriage really took a turn for the better.

KEN: The Lord really dealt with me from that night on as I realised that I can't minister to others if my home life isn't right. Alison was correct, I was so shocked that she was relieved that I had walked out. I expected her to be in floods of tears! I think we were just poles apart and as I learned in my childhood, when you're poles apart, then you fight the bit out. Being raised in a rough area, I learned that you didn't back down, you couldn't be weak. When she spoke to me that night, it really shocked me to the core. Was life so bad with me that she was relieved I was gone?

I knew things had to change. I think the stress of losing my mum, having a wife who wasn't well, being unable to do what I felt I needed to do for the Lord and also financial problems, it was all just mounting up. I didn't just love Alison, I loved the Lord too and somehow I was realising *'The steps of a good man are ordered by the Lord: and he delighteth in his way.'* Psalms 37:23.

Somehow, I was messing my steps up and I knew if I was in the Lord's steps, peace would be in our marriage.

In looking back now, if it hadn't of been for Alison in those first few years, we just wouldn't have had a marriage. She put up with me, even when I was being a real idiot by investing in a false belief that 'ministry' was more important than my wife. She was patient when I was wrong.

You see, I had taken my 'old me' into the marriage, the one that just believed you spoke your mind, the one who got it out, even if it was pure anger, then that's it, it's over. Obviously I know now, that's not how to work within a marriage, especially when you are a new creation in Jesus Christ.

2 Corinthians 5:17; *'Therefore if any man be in Christ, he is a new creature: old things are passed away; behold, all things are become new.'* What is a new creature in Christ but one who has turned from their past life and is living a completely new life by being enabled through the Holy Spirit living in you. Sure we can renounce the devil, we can turn from our sin and turn to Christ, we can leave our old life, our transgressions, our sin and our shortcomings under the blood of Jesus, but we must also leave our old character so that Christ can be glorified through us.

The old man must be crucified afresh and, if, or since the Holy Spirit lives in you, then it just stands to reason that the fruit of the spirit will prevail in our lives over the old nature.

Galatians 5:22-25 reads; *'But the fruit of the Spirit is love, joy, peace, longsuffering, gentleness, goodness, faith, meekness, temperance: against such there is no law. And they that are Christ's have crucified the flesh with the affections and lusts. If we live in the Spirit, let us also walk in the Spirit.'*

Ministry or anniversary...

It was our first wedding anniversary and I wanted to make a special gesture for it so I had spent all day prepping and making dinner for my love, to surprise him when he would arrive home. I had nice romantic music playing in the background, some candles had been lit and his favourite food was ready - chilli. And of course I had removed all my working attire that had the smell of the kitchen and had myself all dressed up, after all, they say; 'dress to impress!'

The front door opened and in Ken walks and I told him that I had prepared a nice meal for us. I brought in a plate of chilli and set it on the table in front of him and then realised I had no cheese on it. I went back into the kitchen and grated some cheese as fast I could but when I came back into the room I was appalled, my heart hit the floor.

Ken had eaten his dinner and left the table making himself comfortable, he was now lying on the sofa with his feet up watching television. I felt like a wet rag, deflated, unloved, unappreciated as I sat on my own eating our anniversary dinner.

I was so annoyed, I said to him; "Why did you just eat that?" He replied; "Sure it was lovely, it didn't need cheese!" What did I learn from that? I learned, if Ken walked into a ministry meeting, or dinner with another minister, he would not have eaten without them. I learned that his chat, his focus, his mannerism would have been so different if another, who wasn't me, was sitting at the table. What we do for others we must do for those who are close at hand also.

Section 6

Faith

'Now faith is the substance of things hoped for, the evidence of things not seen. For by it the elders obtained a good report. Through faith we understand that the worlds were framed by the word of God, so that things which are seen were not made of things which do appear. By faith Abel offered unto God a more excellent sacrifice than Cain, by which he obtained witness that he was righteous, God testifying of his gifts: and by it he being dead yet speaketh. By faith Enoch was translated that he should not see death; and was not found, because God had translated him: for before his translation he had this testimony, that he pleased God. But without faith it is impossible to please him: for he that cometh to God must believe that he is, and that he is a rewarder of them that diligently seek him.'

Hebrews 11:1-6

Chapter Twelve
A calling to the mission field...

I was asked in September 1999, to go to Romania for three weeks. I was anxious about leaving Alison behind but we both knew she wouldn't be fit to go. Her mum agreed to look after her until I returned, so I agreed to go. While we were there, myself and Pastor McConnell took a walk through the village of Carani and he asked me if I would move to Romania to oversee the orphanage that was being set up there and to establish a church for the locals. I told him I would pray about it but the logical part of my head knew that me moving to Romania would never work with Alison.

I did as I said though and I prayed about it, I was praying on the plane on the way home but when I arrived I could see that Alison wasn't doing well at all. I was shocked when I saw how frail she had become even in the time I was away, so I knew she couldn't cope with moving to Romania. I took myself off and told the Lord; "Lord if you want me to go to Romania then you will have to heal her!"

A few weeks passed and we had both been praying about Romania but nothing was improving with Alison so we went and spoke to Pastor McConnell, we told him that we couldn't go. He just looked at me and said; "Aye, aye, just keep praying!" So we went away thinking that we would pray on. We were going to healing meetings but Alison remained the same.

A healing touch...

Prior to my relapse, I hadn't thought about healing. It's not something that you really even hear about in the traditional churches that I was used to. Healing wasn't something I was taught or heard about until I started attending Whitewell. Pastor McConnell had started taking healing meetings on a Tuesday morning and we started to attend them.

It wasn't easy as I had to save my energy, so lots of forward planning was needed. I would make a point to attend on a Tuesday morning, it was in these meetings that I felt I gained strength. Ken had prayed for me, the elders and deacons had anointed me with oil, people fasted and prayed. Nothing changed.

By the time I got ready it looked like I had ran a marathon and needed to start over again but I got myself ready that morning and went to church. It was just a normal service, we sang a couple of songs and we were just coming around the breaking of bread table. Pastor McConnell as he normally would do, started to sing *'Be still and know that I am God.'* We all joined in and sang with him. He sang the second verse, *'I am the God that healeth thee.'* Pastor McConnell then said to us; "If you are here this morning and you are in need, will you stand up and reach out to the Lord? The Lord is here, He is here to touch and He is here to heal."

I hated having to do public displays as I felt everyone would be looking at me, wondering what was wrong. I didn't like putting myself out there as having a problem, but you know what, your need is greater than your pride, so I got myself up. Although I knew that verse of Scripture and had read it, and I knew that the Lord was my healer, it was like I had heard it for the first time. It entered my heart, it was more than just a little chorus. I meant it while I was singing it, but now I felt it. I stood up to sing and I actually thought that Ken had stood up beside me, knowing I didn't like to stand, as I felt a hand on my shoulder. I presumed it was Ken, of course I later found out that I was standing alone. I could feel the heat on my shoulder and the heat then spread through my entire body. I felt strength going into my body and I knew when I was standing there praising the Lord that He had touched me. I just knew something different had happened to me. It was such a nearness of the Lord, such a presence, the heat was intense and it felt like there was an oil pouring over me.

After the service I decided not to share my experience, I wanted to make sure that I was healed. With M.E. you have good days and bad days so I wanted to test it out. I waited, as Pastor McConnell always said to give it three days, then after three days to go and see him. I decided to do just that and see how I felt.

The next day I got up and I felt great, the second day I was up and even did some hoovering. This was a major improvement for me and most of all, I wasn't tired after doing it. Normally, if I had of tried to do some hoovering then I would have paid the price for it for a few days afterwards, but not this time. I felt great.

This just kept continuing and by the third day I just knew - I was healed!

Physically I hadn't tired once, I had this strength and energy and everything within me just knew it was over. I felt completely different, so I told Ken. Of course at this stage he had noticed that I was better, but he hadn't said anything to me. I think he was keeping quiet so I would continue doing the housework! Housework certainly wasn't his area of expertise!

Pastor McConnell always told us this story about going up to Cavehill in Belfast, it overlooks the city and you can see the church from there. He always said it was a great place to go to pray and intercede. He really sells it, he used to say; "It blows the smell off you up there." So I decided that I wanted to go, now I was feeling better, I wanted to go up and see what it was like. Ken looked at me, I knew what he was thinking but I wasn't crazy, I was determined - I knew I could do it. In hindsight I know now it was a silly thing to do as my muscles had weakened. I couldn't manage walking to the end of the street, let alone walking vertically up Cavehill but in my determination, I was doing it. The Pastor always said to do something that you couldn't do before, so I was going up Cavehill!

So away we went, I did make it to the top but the last part I do think Ken had to trail me most of the way, but my determination won the day, I had made it!

At that moment, I hadn't a care in the world, to me I had just done the impossible and it felt good! There was me standing at the top of the Cavehill and for the last year and a half I couldn't even climb the stairs at home! God is good! I knew I was completely healed, miraculously healed. I have never looked back from that moment. God really proved himself to me that in Him - all things are possible.

When I was going to the healing services, the Lord gave me a Scripture. One I could stand strong on, even when I was having a really low day.

'Hast thou not known? hast thou not heard, that the everlasting God, the Lord, the Creator of the ends of the earth, fainteth not, neither is weary? There is no searching of his understanding. He giveth power to the faint; and to them that have no might he increaseth strength. Even the youths shall faint and be weary, and the young men shall utterly fall: But they that wait upon the Lord shall renew their strength; they shall mount up with wings as eagles; they shall run, and not be weary; and they shall walk, and not faint.' Isaiah 40:28-31.

If you are reading this book and are suffering with M.E. or any other disease yourself, I would like to encourage you to believe that there are better days ahead. There were times during my illness when things were very dark, I felt very alone as everyone else was getting on with their own lives, that's the thing when you are ill, life moves on without you. I was stuck. People move on, yes they feel for you but when you can't run alongside them, they soon leave you behind. One of the main things that got me through those times was the Scripture I just shared.

Faith looks to the mornings joy...

Psalm 30:1-5; *'I will extol thee, O Lord; for thou hast lifted me up, and hast not made my foes to rejoice over me. O Lord my God, I cried unto thee, and thou hast healed me. O Lord, thou hast brought up my soul from the grave: thou hast kept me alive, that I should not go down to the pit. Sing unto the Lord, O ye saints of his, and give thanks at the remembrance of his holiness. For his anger endureth but a moment; in his favour is life: weeping may endure for a night, but joy cometh in the morning.'*

This Psalm is one of praise and adoration of the Lord from the heart of David because David has come though many a trial. Many a thing has come upon David to try and discourage him from the ways of the Lord. To try and shift David from following his God. No matter what David had to endure, God always delivered his servant. It was David's faith that looked towards the mornings joy. It was David's faith in his God. Faith looks to the mornings joy. It's through those times of despair, through those times of hurt, through those times of mourning, through times of concern and heartache that our faith always looks towards the mornings joy.

We know there is a future for us in God. We know He has a plan, He has a purpose and that 'morning' will break someday on your horizon. The joy of the morning break will cause you to rejoice as David has in this wonderful Psalm. David lived in the mountains, he lived in caves, he roamed the wilderness when he was being hunted down by his enemies. Now he sees the blessing of the Lord and he is rejoicing that God has been so good to him. All the times of hiding, all the times of fearfulness, night has surely passed. In other words: a season of darkness had covered David's life. It was a season that David never thought he would get out of but his faith always looked to the mornings joy. This is when the Lord would come through and answer his prayers. This is when the Lord breaks forth into our day, into our lives and into our hearts. When the circumstances that are captivating us and taking us into bonds of slavery, those chains are broken and the captives are set free in Christ.

Faith says; "Lord, you are going to bring me through, you are going to make me strong, you are going to heal me." Faith says; "Lord, I am going to make it, you won't let me fall." Faith says; "Lord, you won't let me go, for the morning is coming when Christ will break the clouds and on that great day, joy will be in the hearts of the redeemed."

Psalm 30 is a song of faith. Lord, you have said it, that settles it and I believe it.

Section 7

Obedience; "Yes Lord, send me!"

'And Samuel said, Hath the Lord as great delight in burnt offerings and sacrifices, as in obeying the voice of the Lord? Behold, to obey is better than sacrifice, and to hearken than the fat of rams.'

1 Samuel 15:22

Chapter Thirteen
Getting filled with the Holy Spirit...

As I said, I was praying to God; "Lord if you want me in Romania then you will have to heal Alison."

At the start of November, Alison was healed so we both flew over to Romania to the opening of the orphanage. When we came home, we were still living in Deacon Street. We lived in one of the rooms of the house for three months while the rest of the house was being renovated.

One day, shortly after we came back, I was in the living room seeking the Lord. Alison was out with her mum. I was sitting reading and was looking through the Scriptures asking God to reveal His will to me about Romania. There was a loud rap at the window, it was my friend David. He drove a van picking up people and taking them to work, he came in and he said to me; "I have to do something tonight, could you help me out?"

I said; "No problem, what is it?"

He said; "Will you do my run for me tonight?"

I said; "That's no problem."

So off he went, I went back to my Bible and I just closed it shut, then standing at the end of the living room, I started praying. My prayers turned into singing, I started singing unto the Lord and as I did, I started singing 'hallelujah' and I was praising and shouting as loud as I could. While I was doing this, the Lord baptised me in the Holy Ghost. I started speaking in tongues and I remember the sense of God in the room, He just filled the room and I couldn't stop what I was doing. I was completely caught up in the Spirit, I don't know how long that lasted but then suddenly the window rapped again. It was David and I knew he wouldn't know what was wrong with me, but I went to the door and let him in.

David came in and sat on the settee, I tried to steady myself and sit down on the chair. I knew he was talking to me but I had no idea what he was saying, it was like I wasn't really there. Next thing, I saw another car pull up and it was my brother, he was a backslider. He came in and they were talking to each other but I wasn't really taking in their conversation.

Later on, Alison and her mum arrived back but went on through to the kitchen. Stephen and David were chatting away but as I sat on the chair the Lord started to speak to me. As He did, I thought of all the times I got up early every Sunday morning and walked to Stephen's house to stand outside and pray for him to come back to God. Just then, the Lord spoke to me in a clear voice, He said; "Get up and leave the room, I am bringing Stephen back to me now."

I just got up and went into the kitchen closing the door behind me. Alison and her mum were talking, she asked me if everything was okay. I said that it was. Both of them looked at me as if something was wrong but I told them there was nothing wrong, that Stephen was going to come back to the Lord.

Alison said to me; "Was he talking to David about it?"

I said; "No, God spoke to me about it."

Literally, seconds later the kitchen door opened and Stephen said; "I have something to tell you."

I said to him; "I know, you've come back to the Lord."

And David said to me; "Did you hear us?"

I said; "No, I heard God."

After everyone had left, I went for a walk down the Shore Road towards the park. I was walking and praying.

I said; "Lord, what do you want me to do for you?"

The Lord spoke to me and said; "Will you give everything up for me? Will you give it all away?"

We were in this renovated, newly refurbished house. I knew Alison loved the house, how could I go home and ask her to give it away? Moving from the flat to that house, it was like a palace to both of us. I continued to pray and I asked God to prepare Alison as I expected her to react badly to having to give everything away.

When I arrived back at the house Alison was in the kitchen, she was standing at the cooker with her back to me. I could see her shoulders moving up and down, I didn't know if she was laughing or crying but I soon realised she was crying her eyes out. I was a little stunned as she isn't a weepy person but she was in floods of tears. My heart sank, I thought someone had died. I said to her; "What's going on, love, has something happened?"

She couldn't speak to me, she was so upset. She just pointed towards her little blue King James Bible that her Brethren grandfather had bought her, I didn't understand. I brought her over to the dining table and got her to sit down. She started to calm down a little then eventually she said; "Ken, the Lord has spoken to me, I was reading the Word and the Lord told me, we are to go."

ALISON: After mum had left, Ken went out for a walk so I thought I would have a little quiet time. Ken had been asking me to pray about Romania but I hadn't really asked for a yes or no answer so I thought I would sit down and do that now while I had some peace. I started reading about the woman that came to anoint the Lord with her alabaster box. How she had something really precious but was willing to give it up and how this was to anoint the Lord. I read that and I really felt the Lord beginning to speak to me within that story. From there, I read about Gethsemane and read about the garden.

As I started to read about the garden, it was like I could see a little movie in my mind. I could see the Lord telling the disciples to watch and pray, lest they would fall into temptation. Then it said this, *'And he went a little farther, and fell on his face.'* (Matthew 26:39) As I read that, I could see it, I could see my Lord falling on His face. And in that, I asked the Lord; "Why? Why did you do that?" And this voice spoke straight to my heart; "For you." That completely broke me, I just wept and wept. I was broken at the idea that the Lord had carried that burden, He fell on his face and did that for me. I read the next part which was; *'O my Father, if it be possible, let this cup pass from me: nevertheless not as I will, but as thou wilt.'* Matthew 26:39.

It was my will to stay in my nice new home, it was my will to start a family here in Northern Ireland but it was God's will that I had to surrender my will to His. So, I told God, if Romania was where He wanted me, then that was it, I would go. I had such a reality of surrendering my will to God and was just such a mess when Ken came in. I was standing in the kitchen trying to compose myself, to get the dinner on. So whenever Ken told me that he felt God wanted us to give all away to go to Romania, it wasn't an issue, as far as I was concerned - it was already done. The Lord had dealt with me.

Alison and I went to visit Pastor McConnell and told him that we were going to Romania and he was pleased. We then started giving away all our possessions, we blessed people with everything we had, including our car. We kept a few personal items, special wedding gifts that were personal to us and that nobody else would want, but we were told to give it all away and so we did. We were very much both in agreement that we had to be obedient, if God told us to give it all away then that was exactly what we would do. We didn't want to be holding on to things just in case it didn't work out. As it says in 1 Samuel 15:22; *'And Samuel said, Hath the Lord as great delight in burnt offerings and sacrifices, as in obeying the voice of the Lord? Behold, to obey is better than sacrifice, and to hearken than the fat of rams.'*

We were very torn about our new shiny home but it wasn't to be kept as a back-up plan if things were difficult in Romania. We were going to be missionaries and we were going to do it properly, we were going to make a new life for ourselves over there. I wasn't going to be like Ananias and Sapphira (Acts 5) who only brought half their possessions and sold half. As far as I was concerned this was going to be us for life, so I was going to be fully obedient to God. Things seemed to move very quickly after that and we were away to start a new season of our lives in Romania.

Life in Romania...

Romania was a culture shock. I was homesick a lot. I left my father who was now alone in his house and I knew he didn't want me to go. Because God calls you, it doesn't mean it's always going to be easy. We were about to have our beautiful, believer, rose-tinted glasses cracked and smashed!

We chose the call of Christ and that call brought us hard and difficult times which became a fiery furnace but as with the three Hebrew boys in Daniel 3, Christ was the fourth man in the fire. And so, He was with us in ours also. Although we didn't fully realise it at times and couldn't understand it, yet He was. He keeps his word, He keeps his promises. As the Scripture says in Matthew 8:20; *'Lo, I am with you always, even unto the end of the world.'* He remains faithful.

We were so unqualified but found out that the trial of our faith was much more precious than that of gold that perishes. God doesn't call the qualified but rather He qualifies the called and although we can't see Him, yet we love Him and in it all then obey him by dying to self. When serving Him in that call because of love and the great gratitude to Him for all that He has done, we rejoice with joy unspeakable and full of glory.

We have learned to trust in Him, rest in His grace, bow and bend to his sovereignty and understand when there is no comprehension that He is in it and in all things, God works together for the good. As it says in Romans 8:28; *And we know that all things work together for good to them that love God, to them who are called according to his purpose.'*

Even in the hardest, darkest moves and the most terrible times, a dark season is never controlled by the devil. A dark season is God's path to bring the saint to a greater light. Jesus is the Almighty, he rules every situation.

I didn't like Romania at all but when I kept myself busy it was okay. As a young couple, there was no privacy. It was all shared living. We did have a bedroom to ourselves so this was the only place we could go to talk privately or to have time together. Even at that, the living room was next to our room so you always felt like there was people with you. We were just constantly surrounded by people and they were in our space, you couldn't have found five minutes so it was a big change in lots of different ways.

There was a small meeting opened with many children and this increased. I was told that if I opened the church, they would arrest me. So I went ahead.

We then encountered a lot of opposition in Romania from the other churches and beliefs. We were not popular with the Greek Orthodox church and we were followed almost daily by the Jehovah Witnesses. If I walked around speaking to people and going door to door, they would have done the same, asking the people what I had been saying.

We carried on, Alison mostly helped in the orphanage but I wanted to grow the church so I went with an interpreter to a printing shop to get some leaflets made, I thought I could then go door to door and spread the news about Jesus. But before I even got back with the flyers, one was delivered to the office with a note attached saying that if they were distributed, I would be put in prison. Needless to say, I carried on regardless but the opposition was great.

I remember one day I had just delivered some wood into one of the areas, for their fires at home, along with some bread. The people were delighted. I had filled up a small wood shed so they could have heat and the next thing I knew, I just saw this flash, somebody had ran out of the crowd with an iron bar and knocked me out. I fell to the ground but the people gathered around me and protected me. I got up with a huge bump on my head. The people were concerned, they said that I should maybe stop helping them as they didn't want me getting hurt. I wasn't going to stop anything – we were there for Christ's Kingdom. I wasn't going to be intimidated.

The more we were challenged, the more we trusted God. The Lord started moving and the people were blessed. We were then able to pray for the people and we were seeing people being healed. In the orphanage, we witnessed restoration as families were reunited. It was the Lord at work.

At the orphanage, we had opened up the church at the front. There was a little house which used to be a Baptist meeting house, it was converted and cleaned up. I had been round the houses, going door to door to try and get the people to come to church. One Sunday morning, I was ready for church. I walked out from the orphanage towards the church. We had a back entrance that took us into the building instead of the door in from the street. Usually people started arriving around 10.45am for the service to begin at 11am. It was around this time that I walked in through the back entrance to the church and there wasn't one person there!

I couldn't believe it, I had worked so hard especially in the previous three weeks to build relationships with the people. I had brought them aid, labouring, trying to reach them day in and day out and here I was and there wasn't one person.

I walked out through the church onto the street and I remember it was a lovely sunny morning. Right outside the church door is the one road that goes through all the villages. It was the main road but it was a real rough, bumpy road. Opposite the church was two houses with a gap in between them. I was standing and I was so dejected, it was now ten minutes until church was to begin and there wasn't a sign of anybody on the street.

The street was empty – not a person. It was like a ghost town, it was terrible. I looked up and down, nobody about. I looked across the road and in between the two houses was this wee black dot. It was something small and black coming towards me. I realised it was a little bird. It really caught my attention, it was coming towards me flying and swooping like a sparrow.

Just at that moment, I could hear a car coming. That was very unusual as very few people in the village drove cars, I watched and this car appeared round the bend on the road and came down past the church. Just as it came near me, the bird I had been watching swooped and the car hit it. The little sparrow landed right at my feet. I looked at it, it was dead. I felt sorry for it, poor wee bird. The Scripture from Matthew 10:29 came to me about the sparrow; *'One of them shall not fall on the ground without your Father knowing.'* I had been sitting thinking, here I am Lord, in Romania, feeling homesick, feeling dejected, defeated. No one even really knew where we were – they hadn't heard of this village, Carani.

Here I was on this Sunday morning and nobody had turned up, this wee bird falls dead at my feet and as bad as I felt for that little sparrow, I turned on my heels and walked round the back of the church towards the orphanage, through the side entry. I walked into the orphanage and I sat and I cried unto God. I said; "Nobody is coming Lord, you know all about it. Nothing is happening, I am going to leave this in your hands."

It took me five or ten minutes to settle myself, I then got up and decided to go into the church to lock it up. I walked down the yard and into the church and when I arrived, the church was packed! People must have flocked into it within the last ten minutes. I am sure my face was a picture as I was absolutely gobsmacked! I had just opened the door on chaos, there were people and children everywhere – I couldn't believe my eyes!

I had settled that even though it seemed all was lost and I was wondering; "Where are you Lord? Do you even know I am here? do you even know where I am, as nobody knows where Carani is?" I settled that God knew about it and I had left it that as He knew about it, He would do what He wanted to do with it. If that meant nothing then that was okay, I would yield myself to that. I had just left it all in His sovereign will. I told Him that I was just leaving it to Him, no matter who turns up or who doesn't. When I got to that church – there wasn't a seat left! It was packed!

It's important for me to add here that the vital lesson I learned and have taken to heart is, wherever you are, however the struggle, whatever the need, if our Father in Heaven can see the little sparrow fair among many millions of sparrows around the world. If He notices it's loss of life, it's demise in falling to the ground, then He sees you, hears your cry, knows you, knows where you are, geographically, mentally, spiritually and physically. You are not out of His reach nor His care.

- **He counts your steps;** *'For now thou numberest my steps.'* Job 14:16.

- **He numbers your hairs;** *'But even the very hairs of your head are all numbered. Fear not therefore: ye are of more value than many sparrows.'* Luke 12:7.

- He knows your ways, bottles your tears and writes it down; *'Thou tellest my wanderings: put thou my tears into thy bottle: are they not in thy book?'* Psalm 56:8.

- He is your guide and He satisfies; *'And the Lord shall guide thee continually, and satisfy thy soul in drought, and make fat thy bones: and thou shalt be like a watered garden, and like a spring of water, whose waters fail not.'* Isaiah 58:11.

- He is your best friend; *'And there is a friend that sticketh closer than a brother.'* Proverbs 18:24.

You are worth more than many sparrows. He is your omniscient, omnipotent and omnipresent Father. Place your all, your hope and your trust in Him. He will make a way where there seems to be no way.

Chapter Fourteen
Dire conditions...

When I arrived at the church, Ken was nowhere to be seen but people were starting to arrive. I was helping organise the children and saw a bus pull up outside, one of the local men had collected a family we had been helping. They lived in absolute squalor, you wouldn't house animals in the place that was their home. It was an old cottage which was literally held together by mud. There were twenty members of a family that lived in it and we met them and I was so horrified that they had nothing, absolutely nothing.

They had all these kids and they had nothing on their feet. Their feet were all cut as they walked everywhere and had never had any shoes. I love kids and couldn't stand to see them suffer so we got the bus driver to take us all into the markets and we bought them all trainers. They were cheap to us but they thought they were really expensive. Ken then went and got them groceries. They had really bad coughs as they had a fire in the house, it was like a wood burner but the flue had gone in it so it just filled the house with smoke. There were only two rooms in the house but they were filled with thick smoke. The parents asked us for cough medicine but it was clear the coughing was because of the smoke. We got the flue fixed and within days the coughing had stopped. The bus arrived full of this family all in their new trainers. They still went everywhere in their bare feet but wore their trainers on a Sunday as they wanted to keep them good. The church filled up really quickly and then Ken came in through the back door and his face was a picture – just priceless!

I spent most of my time in Romania working with the children. They were just amazing, they had absolutely nothing and they just thrived when you showed them love. I remember one day I said my goodbyes to them as I was going into town with Ken to get a few things. When we returned, I got an awful shock – the place absolutely stank of petrol. Tony, our bus driver was sitting smoking away and all I could smell was petrol! I asked him what was going on. He explained that the kids had head lice so they dunked their heads in petrol. So here were approximately thirty children sitting with their hair saturated in petrol and him sitting beside them smoking away! We yelled at him to get out! I was horrified! I had head lice ointment in the cupboards but as I wasn't there, they just used what they knew – petrol. Their wee heads were soaking in it, I couldn't believe my eyes. My eyes were actually smarting just being near them. I had to get them all washed, I was really frightened by this treatment of the children.

KEN: There was a little girl who had a big split between her toes and right up her feet. She really needed medical attention as the foot was open, it needed stitched. We were very concerned about her health as she had a serious problem with her foot and she like the others, were living in squalor. At home, we wouldn't get away with keeping pigs in those conditions and here was another family who had absolutely nothing. They were filthy and the house stank of smoke from the fire. This little girl's mummy was pregnant again and it was just awful.

We went to the shops and bought them groceries and some soap. That lady was so delighted to get soap powder, it was something she could never afford. She had wanted to keep her family clean but just had no money to do so. That family came to the Lord too. We went back and forward to them and helped them in any way we could. When she had her new baby she actually called her Alison. She must be the only one in Romania with that name.

Reaching the people...

There was a wee man that used to sit on the street and he couldn't hear anything and the kids used to torture him. They used to come up behind him and scare him. He was only a small man and the kids used to jump at him and call him names. One day I met him and I discovered he wasn't deaf but he just needed a battery for his hearing aid but he couldn't afford one. They were also nearly impossible to get in Romania.

I sent word home and shortly afterwards I received a matchbox in the post with hearing aid batteries inside. I put a battery into his ear and a few days later he came to me and said; "I now feel like a man and the kids can't jump out on me any more – I can hear them!"

I was blown away that such a simple thing made this man feel like a man. It was amazing. I spent time talking with him and he gave his life to the Lord.

I remember one day in particular, I was walking around the streets doing some evangelism and all around me I could hear pigs squealing, it was deafening at times. I asked one of the men, why they were squealing like that. Sometimes I watched them chasing them up the street with a stick. But he said that they knew their fate – they were going to be butchered.

This day, I was out on the streets and I came across a gateway, I could see a group of men and women around a table with their backs to me. Through the interpreter, we started a conversation and they invited me to come over to them. When I went over to them I could see two large tables, they were thick like butchers' tables. They had just slaughtered a pig and they collected the pig's blood to use as a black pudding, they called it a blood pudding. They had huge basins on the ground full of water. They were taking the intestines out of the pig.

They wrapped the intestine around their finger, they emptied the contents into the first bucket of dirty water then they blew it like a balloon. That was their sausage skin.

The pig's back was laying on the table, the table was full of blood and guts, it was a gruesome sight. I was chatting away to them, trying to get them to come to church. I was telling them about the gospel and they were speaking back to me through the interpreter. I could see they were pretty hard, they just didn't want to know. One of the men put his finger up to me as if he was saying 'one minute' and I watched as he brought out a small knife, it looked like a letter opener. He put it under the subcutaneous skin of the pig's back that was laying there and he cut a rectangular piece of skin out.

He rolled it up into a size of a pencil then he got a handful of salt and rolled it in it. His hands were filthy with gutting the pig so the salt was clung to his bloody hands.

He threw it onto the table and it was soaking up everything. He turned to me and he handed it to me as if he wanted me to eat it. I said; "No, no thank you."

I looked at my interpreter, I asked him; "Surely he doesn't want me to eat that?"

He said to me; "Yes, he does, it is a delicacy. They use it to chew on while they talk."

I said; "Tell him my dinner is nearly ready but thank him very much." But the man insisted even more that I would eat it.

The interpreter said to me; "He really wants you to eat it, he is offended." I didn't even eat pork so the thought of eating pig skin certainly did not appeal. It was a very hard situation. The interpreter tried to talk to him but he wasn't having it, he said to me; "Do you want to win the people or not?"

I said; "I do."

He said; "Eat it."

So I took a deep breath and I ate it. It was one of the worst experiences of my life. It tasted like salty rubber, I had never tasted anything quite like it. It was absolutely rotten.

The man was delighted, he said to me; "Plăcut, plăcut" which means 'nice, nice.'

I said; "Yes, tell him thanks very much." He went to cut me another piece so I said; "No, no I have to go now."

I took quite ill after that, I ended up in a private clinic in the city getting tests done. I was very weak, they thought I had an infection which had spread to my lung. I went back to the church and got the people to lay hands on me and the Lord healed me, I never looked back.

Chapter Fifteen
A house divided...

As shared in the last chapter, those were only some of the wonderful things we saw God do in Romania and yet in the midst of this time, as sure as night versus day, opposition arose.

Paul wrote in 2 Corinthians 2:11; *'Lest Satan should get an advantage of us: for we are not ignorant of his devices.'*

God's plan for our lives as the Church, is *'that they* (you and me) *may be one, even as we are one,'* John 17:23. Against the backdrop of this, the devil will do his utmost to stop us being as one with each other through disunity. We must always ask, are we in strife, gossip, backbiting with your brother or sister in the Lord?

As Christians, our life and what we say and do, should glorify the Lord. In other words, what would Christ do?

Alison and I could easily share of how we sacrificed our life in Northern Ireland to go to a foreign land at the time, to only find out it would be cut short by accusation. But in truth, would we have changed a moment of what took place against us? No! For each experience in this life we can either let it knock us down, or seek to take us to another level of character building and a greater understanding in our walk in Christ.

But I have realised that it is one thing to write about it from outside the situation now, but another to be walking through it.

For me, the goal had been set for us to build a work in Romania and now it was all going wrong for us, we thought.

Even with all the good things that were taking place in Romania, word was sent to us. We had to return back home.

When we got back to Belfast we went to see Pastor McConnell. It was then we found out that false reports had been sent back to him. We were shocked and devastated, as both the Pastor and ourselves were unaware of many of the things that was actually happening. Yes, we knew of ongoing strife in the camp in Romania but the decision had been made to take the higher ground and put aside any indifference for the sake of the gospel for a divided house cannot stand. (Mark 3:24-25)

Scripture teaches us; *'Behold, how good and how pleasant it is for brethren to dwell together in unity! It is like the precious ointment upon the head, that ran down upon the beard, even Aaron's beard: that went down to the skirts of his garments; As the dew of Hermon, and as the dew that descended upon the mountains of Zion: for there the Lord commanded the blessing, even life for evermore.'* Psalms 133:1-3.

One has to fight for unity and it starts with a decision to love one and another, to seek the best for each other, to put another before you!

The door to Romania was now well closed and for us, we had swapped the closure of it, for unity of the body. Instead of complaining and letting it fester, instead of seeking to justify our actions. We decided to live in the spirit of unity.

We knew we must do what is right no matter what people would think or say.

ALISON: I had just packed a bag each for us to come back, with clothes for our stay in Belfast, all our personal possessions were still in Romania. I couldn't believe what was happening. I cried as I thought of all the little children I had worked with, I wouldn't get to say goodbye. We were shell-shocked, as in Romania we were informed that we were going home for a holiday, to be then told when we arrived home, that we were back for good.

We didn't know what our next natural step was. We moved in with Ken's brother and his wife for a few weeks. Then we moved to a small bedsit in east Belfast for three months, then to Donaghcloney.

With not really knowing what had just happened. One minute we were in the call of God in Romania then we were where?

The stress of the whole situation made Ken really ill as at night he would wake up with his pillow having blood on it. His body was aching all over and his mood was very low. His skin was shedding and his body was out in ulcers and blisters. It got to the stage that the pain was causing him not to walk properly and he was sent to the arthritis clinic in Belfast. The hospital began tests for bone cancer. Because of this, we discovered that he was Coeliac.

Suddenly, I became his carer.

It went from him needing to be dressed, to the point he would sit all day staring at the wall, not feeding himself. Wherever he sat in the morning when I left to work in the nursing home, that is exactly where I would find him on my return. Ken was having a breakdown.

It's difficult to walk straight when you know others are talking down about you. But friend, sometimes you just need to look into that mirror and say, "Arise woman/man of God!" Especially when you know you are the one who was not in the wrong.

I was sitting reading one day and I came across the story in Ruth 2:8, where Boaz said to Ruth, '...*Go not to glean in another field...*' I was thinking; "I am finished with this church and I am off to look for another place to worship to glean, to be fed." But the Lord through his Word spoke to me and said; '*Go not to glean in another field, nether go from thence, but abide here fast by my maidens.*' Meaning, stay close to them, don't go to another place.

My first reaction was, what about my feelings, what about my hurt, what about my loss, what about me, Lord?

I soon learned that my flesh seeks to feel sorry for itself, but the good news is, I died that Christ might live through me, I died when I got saved. It's no longer I that liveth, as it says in Galatians 2:20; '*I am crucified with Christ: nevertheless I live; yet not I, but Christ liveth in me: and the life which I now live in the flesh I live by the faith of the Son of God, who loved me, and gave himself for me.*'

When I said to the Lord; "What about my loss, what about our loss?" As I said these words, the words came; "Really, Ken?"

The breakdown was because I could not see a way out and now God was showing me His path.

I needed now to stop focusing on me and my loss. I came with nothing into this world and if I leave with nothing only Christ, all things of this earth is worthless in comparison to having Jesus.

Peter was a man like many of us. One day, he sees what no other sees by announcing, '*Thou art Christ the Son of the living God.*' (Matthew 16:16) A short time later, a rooster was crowing announcing, '*You've missed the mark!* (Matthew 26:34) Yet Peter like me, makes a pity-party statement and says, '*Lo, we have left all, and followed thee.*' But Jesus immediately shines a light onto the darkness that was surrounding Peter's understanding... '*And he* (Jesus) *said unto them, Verily I say unto you, There is no man the kingdom of God's sake, Who shall not receive manifold more in this present time, and in the world to come life everlasting.*' Luke 18:28-30.

Imagine the audacity, the vanity and the ignorance of someone like me saying that to Jesus as Peter just said; "We have left all." What an insult it must be to the generous giving, gracious God of heaven. He who left glory to come to this sin-cursed earth!

He who came from the worship and adoration of the angels to be taunted, mocked, scorned, beaten and crucified by man. He who is the Almighty, humbled Himself to be clothed in flesh and to be taken by the feeble, by the frail hands of sinful men whose breath is in their nostrils. He who is the fountain of life and The Life of all living things, gave up His life for a vile, wretch like me, need I say any more?

And we complain by reminding Him we have left all, oh forgive us Lord how we can place any worldly goods against the sacrifice of Your life.

Let us remind ourselves in James 1:17; *'Every good gift and every perfect gift is from above, and cometh down from the Father of lights, with whom is no variableness, neither shadow of turning.'*

Again, would I obey Plan A; the Word He spoke to me, or would I go for the easier option of Plan B? Cut and run to glean in another field! In truth, Plan B should NEVER be an option. For His plan for you, plan A, the Alpha and Omega plan is always good!

For Ruth, Plan B showed; if she had left and went to another field, then she was just bringing her burden to another place and to another people and so would I. As the saying goes... far off fields are green! But are they?

God's instruction to me was - to stay and watch Him work.

Boaz ordered handfuls of grain to fall on purpose (Ruth 2:16) and that's what we got until things came into full light.

God had said in Ruth 2:8; *'Abide here fast by my maidens.'* In other words, stay close, get even closer to my maidens. In spite of how I think or feel, they are God's maidens of His people. The lesson to learn is, we all make mistakes.

We can place people on a pedestal and sad to say, it is us who puts them there in our minds. Then when the smallest of our expectations are not met we become discouraged. Leaders who have fed you, led you, prayed with you and stayed with you throughout many difficult times. Stood with you through dangers and disasters all of a sudden went from being your hero to your zero, through their human weakness. Never forget those who stand with you in your dark season, for anyone can stand with you when the light is on!

After praying and studying this Scripture, I said to Alison, that I really felt the Lord was telling me to stay put, to go from enduring to enjoying the family of believers again.

This was where the Lord had planted me, so this is where I should stay. And that is exactly what the Lord did, from then on, He gave us handfuls on purpose.

The Lord spoke to me in Romans 16:20; *'And the God of peace shall bruise satan under your feet shortly.'* That word 'shortly' really stood out to us.

Slowly but surely, truth after truth came out of what took place in Romania. It was God who now was fighting our battles.

What we gave away to go to Romania, it was all restored to us as people came around us to help.

Chapter Sixteen
Entering Beulah Land...

The children in Romania had stolen my heart, and feeling bereft, I believed it was time for Ken and I to have our own children.

Like Hannah in 1 Samuel 1, I was also struggling to become pregnant, I went into a downward spiral in my mind.

Time passed and one day as I was praying, the Lord gave me a verse of Scripture in Psalm 127:3; *'Lo, children are an heritage of the Lord: and the fruit of the womb is his reward.'* As I read this, I felt that I would be rewarded for my obedience in Romania. It was coming up to Christmas and I was praying; "Lord, all I want for Christmas is to be pregnant."

Shortly into the New Year I was working in the nursing home and as I was hoisting one of the patients up, I took a dizzy spell and fainted. The nurse placed smelling salts under my nose and I came around. She was really worried, she said to me; "Oh Alison, do you think this is your M.E. coming back again?"

I said; "Oh no, no, no, I am healed, it can't be that!" Then it slowly started to dawn on me what it could be... was this pregnancy?

That day after work, I bought a pregnancy test and yes, it was positive!

When I told Ken, his reaction was shock, pure shock! In fact, he was dumbfounded, so much so that he made me do a second pregnancy test, as he didn't believe it. It also showed positive.

KEN: I remember it was a sunny day so I walked down to the nursing home to meet Alison after she finished work. When I arrived a couple of the staff told me that she wasn't feeling well, that she had fainted but to be honest, it never even dawned on me what could be wrong, I was in for a shock!

It was the next day when she told me she had taken a pregnancy test, I nearly fainted myself! I was so shocked. I felt like I had entered another realm. I remember my head just zoning out and when I came round, I was like did I hear that right?

I couldn't believe it so another test was ordered and came back with the same result. Like most men it takes a while for it to settle into our brains... But I was over the moon!

One Sunday morning, it was about 6am and I knew I was in the first stages of labour. I knew this was definitely it but I wasn't fussing as I had been told it could take a whole day. The pains were coming steadily but slowly. By 9am I knew the pains were coming quicker so I rang the hospital and they told me to come in for a check and they would see what was happening.

I had a few other things to put in my bag, I wasn't really rushing myself. I said to Ken; "Ken, this is it, the baby is coming today." He quickly pulled on his tracksuit bottoms and started saying to me; "Come on, come on!" He got himself in a real flap! I told him he could go and take a shower as we had plenty of time as the baby mightn't come until tonight, so off he went.

I had just finished gathering everything I needed when Ken reappeared, freshly washed but he was dressed in his three-piece suit! I was really shocked, a bit overkill for the maternity ward I thought!

I said to him; "Where are you going?"

Ken said; "Well if the child isn't coming, I can go to morning church." Sensitive he was not, I was totally dumbfounded.

I said to him; "We still have to go to the hospital and you need something sensible to wear." Not sure what he was doing but it felt like four hours later, finally Ken was redressed and ready to go to the hospital.

When we arrived at the hospital, the staff gave me some drugs. An experience I will never forget. Here is me in labour and what did they give me? Two co-codamol! What? But yes, that's what they gave me, and into the maternity ward they wheeled me.

Because things were moving so quickly, I didn't have time to get anything else but gas and air, so I wasn't happy. I thought that if I wasn't going to get any other pain relief then I wouldn't use the gas and air until it was really bad. Just shows my naivety at the time! The midwife kept warning me to use the gas and air but I wouldn't listen. I was pacing myself, I told her I would use it when I couldn't cope but she warned me to suck it in whether I needed it or not!

KEN: I remember there was a small tape player above the bed, we were supposed to bring some cassettes to play for labour but all we had was the Whitewell choir. Alison was sucking gas and air and the Whitewell choir was singing 'Beulah Land.' It was as if the glory was about to enter the room and I remember the lyrics were; 'Beulah Land. I'm longing for you, and some day, on thee I'll stand!' Just at that moment, Alison took off her mask and said to me; "I feel like I'm in Beulah Land now!"

I thought she was away with the fairies and I was so nervous, I asked her if I could have a go!

At the final part of labour, Jodie was born. She was 6lb1oz and everything seemed to be good with her but the afterbirth never came. The midwives started telling me that I would have to go for an operation. I wasn't having it, I told them that I had already had my baby, there was no way I was going for an operation now. I was starting to get upset, after all I had been through, I didn't want to be knocked out now for an operation. I looked to Ken and told him to do something! I don't know what I expected him to do but I needed him to fix it!

KEN: I was standing with Jodie in a blanket and the doctor was ordering a nurse to go and get the anaesthetist ready for surgery. Alison was getting really upset, she didn't want an operation. I was pacing back and forth with Jodie who was crying, I didn't know what I was supposed to do but I knew Alison didn't want to go to theatre.

As I was trying to soothe Jodie, I felt the Lord spoke to me, He said; "Go lay your hands on her and pray and I will do this now." As I paced back and forth, these words kept coming to me; 'exercise your faith' and guess what? I didn't.

I thought this is crazy, here is a squealing child in my arms, my wife is upset, doctors are here, the anaesthetist is getting prepared, and yet the Lord wants me to lay my hands on her and say what?! I just refused to do anything, it felt like time was moving really slowly but it was only a few minutes. I just couldn't do it. Two midwives came in at that point and started working with Alison, explaining the procedure. Such conviction came over my heart, it was tangible. I felt that I had really let Alison down and felt disobedient towards the Lord.

One of the midwives left to go to theatre and I remember at that point wrestling with the Lord. I was really struggling... "What if this is just me?" "What if I just look like a fool?" All these questions were going around in my head. It got to the stage where I just said; "Lord, if the doctor was here and I got another chance, then I would do it." Of course, the doctor walked in and said to Alison that they would try again to deliver the afterbirth naturally. He was accompanied by a different midwife, she came in and looked at me and said; "I know you, I recognise your face." I couldn't think who she was at all but after she studied me, she said; "You came and preached at our church one Saturday night in Cookstown." Then it dawned on me who she was.

She then said; "You need to pray!" I couldn't believe it! I told her I was praying. She said to me; "You pray and I will pray."

The doctor turned to us and said that nothing was happening. So I had to step up. I put my hand on Alison's tummy and I said aloud; "Lord, you said to pray for my wife and you would do this. You have told us that where two or more are gathered and agree and touch anything on earth, it will be done according to your will, I believe this is your will."

At that point, everything came away.

The doctor looked at the midwife and he said; "Go and tell them to cancel the theatre and the anaesthetist."

It turned out afterwards, the midwife was called into the office as they wanted to know what had happened. She told them that we prayed and the Lord moved but obviously the hospital staff wouldn't believe that.

It really taught me a lesson that day, my disobedience was going to cause my wife to have an operation. It really showed me that even in the midst of chaos, God can still speak. In the midst of chaos, the storm can be stilled by His Word.

Shortly after Jodie was born, we moved back to Deacon Street in Belfast. Jodie was only 16 months old when I became pregnant again with baby number two. Ken was just as shocked about this pregnancy as he was the first time around. To be honest, I was surprised too at how quickly I became pregnant again.

Ken had really taken to being a father, though he became a real fuss-pot! He used to take a thermometer into all the rooms, then he would tell me if it wasn't the right temperature for Jodie. The heat was adjusted up and down several times a day! I was starting to become concerned what it might become like with another baby!

He was so protective of her, sometimes it was stopping me in my duties as her mummy. If I was going to bathe Jodie, Ken would have to check and triple-check the water before she was allowed in etc. It was certainly a new side to Ken that I hadn't experienced before.

Forgiveness...

After the hurt of Romania, we had to learn to forgive so that we could move on. We knew that if we didn't forgive, the bitterness and anger would have eaten us up. It got to the point where we had to say; "Okay Lord, we leave these people in your hands to deal with and you're going to have to deal with them however you deem fit."

We never tried to vindicate ourselves, it was very difficult but I knew that the Lord would clear us.

Forgiveness is a subject much debated and probably the most difficult in most cases to do. In Matthew chapter 18, Jesus speaks about the man unable to pay a debt but was freely forgiven who then went out and wasn't very forgiving to another who owed a great debt to him. The idea being, you owed a debt you couldn't pay and were forgiven so likewise do the same. This would play very heavy on me; "But Lord!" I would say. "No buts." He would reply.

Forgiveness comes through repentance, yes it does! Luke 13:3; *'Except ye repent, ye shall all likewise perish.'* "But no one has repented yet Lord!" Yes, but none can know the relief of forgiveness until they receive it through the repentance and confessing of their fault. But, you can forgive in the midst of hurt, even in your innocence of the situation and let God deal with it, so a root of bitterness does not take hold of your soul. Luke 23:34; *'Then said Jesus, Father, forgive them; for they know not what they do.'*

Forgiveness was a command, again He was forgiving me, forgiving us to further us on in Him and His work. The trial of forgiving is like fire, it may burn badly but it will take the impurities and the dross out of your life. That your faith might flourish. Remember when going through times of adversity, a diamond used to be a lump of coal which was compressed and put under intense pressure for many years.

Nearly 16 years later I was sitting in my study and the phone rang. It was the person who caused the trouble for us in Romania. They had rung to ask forgiveness. In that conversation every part of me did not want to forgive and yet when I look at my own sin and Christ forgiving me, who am I to hold debt over another. Each crossroads in life is a choice for us becoming more like Christ and that phone call was another decision I had to make – to hold debt or let go! For those who have wronged you I pray you also will see God's way is letting go and as we let go, our season of bitterness can change into something sweet in the Lord. Is it any wonder Scripture says, *'Taste and see that the Lord is good!'* Psalms 34:8

Chapter Seventeen
Dublin...

Through time, my health started to improve and I got involved in the work in Whitewell again. At that time Pastor McConnell was starting to have rallies in Dublin so I went along and helped out. We were doing a Bible study on a Tuesday night and there was a good response. A year and a half later, we were walking down Dawson Street in the city and Pastor McConnell said; "I think you are the man for here." I wasn't sure but I prayed about it. I didn't feel that I was particularly called to go but I saw the need.

Weeks later I arrived early for the Bible study, I was sitting on the front row and I started to read my Bible while waiting. I felt led to turn to Psalm 32. As I read through the text, I came to verse eight and it said; *'I will instruct thee and teach thee in the way that thou shalt go: I will guide thee with mine eye.'* It was like this one verse was illuminated in the page and I just knew that God was speaking to me, that He would guide me, no matter what I do or where I go. That He would show me the path, this truth was washing over me, it was so real to me.

This elderly lady came along, she was a lovely, godly woman. She sat down on the seat beside me. She said; "Hello, Ken."

I closed my Bible but kept my finger on the page I was reading. She looked at me and said; "Sorry, am I disturbing you?"

I said; "No, not at all. I was just reading something."

She asked what I was reading. I reopened the Bible and showed her. She said; "Oh, Psalm 32?"

I said; "Yes."

"Oh" She said; "Let me tell you a story about Psalm 32."

She told me that she had been offered a job in ministry years ago and she didn't know whether to go or not. She received the Scripture Psalm 32, she then referred to verse eight and told me that the Lord told her, that if she went, He would go with her. I was shocked, everything that I had just been sitting musing on this last few minutes, this lady was telling me the same thing nearly word for word. I was amazed. I closed the Bible and thought it over, everything within me didn't want to go to Dublin.

I just couldn't understand why I had to go through this again and why could the Lord not send us somewhere handier?

Dublin was very much in my mind as I knew the pastor wanted me to go. After the Bible study that night, I went down to Pastor McConnell's house and we went for a walk down the Shore Road together and talked it over. When he was asking me about it, I told him that I didn't feel I was called to go but I did know that if I went, then the Lord would be with me.

Pastor McConnell asked me to give him two years and I agreed, we would go and whether it was right or wrong it was a stepping stone for us in ministry. I didn't realise God had laid down this path for us. It was a path that was difficult at times but it was His way. There were a lot of trials in Dublin but God did bless us through it.

A separate calling?...

In all the rest of the journeys we were on, I had felt the Lord calling me alongside Ken. Obviously it was a separate calling but it was a calling for the two of us. I always would have had the same draw to the place or the situation like Ken.

In Dublin at this time I had my daughter Jodie and was pregnant with our second child so to be honest, my priority was setting up home. Not to be going to Dublin to set up a church away from my family.

I felt no calling to go to Dublin, the Lord didn't speak to me about going and I remember one of the pastors in the church saying to me; "Well, could you support Ken as you would if he was in any other job?" I said; "Yes, absolutely I can do that."

But this was the first time, I felt I had nothing personally to involve myself in. I felt I was just supporting Ken in that work but it wasn't a joint ministry as such. I tried but my heart wasn't really in it.

I felt Dublin was very impractical for this stage of our lives. I was heavily pregnant and had a toddler to care for so we stayed living in Belfast and we commuted up and down to Dublin for the next three months, then Ken was to be ordained as the pastor of the church there.

They set aside a date for Ken's ordination and of course I went into labour! I had went over so in theory, I should have had it all over me but baby Ellie had other ideas.

Ellie was eventually born on 20th September 2003, in the early hours of Saturday morning and Ken's ordination was the next day, on the 21st, so I knew I was going to miss it.

Ken was his usual helpful self in the labour ward and spent his time with his head in his hands praying and my mother who was there wasn't much better as she cried the whole way through it. It was all worth it though as Ellie was a beautiful baby girl with dark hair and rosy red lips.

I was so thankful that Ken was able to be there for Ellie's birth as he had to leave to take the Sunday service in Dublin, which meant he also was unable to bring Ellie and I home from the hospital, so mum came and got us.

Ken's ordination service was that same evening in Whitewell Metropolitan Tabernacle. Ken was bringing a coach load of people from the Dublin church up and on his way decided to stop, yes you got it, at our house to show off our new addition. I was just back and had sat down when I got the shock of my life! I was just after giving birth, I was pale, tired, exhausted and feeling terrible and the coach pulls up to let Ken and everyone else see Ellie... and me!

I was disappointed that I missed the service that evening and so was Ken but nature dictated things differently on this occasion, but the joy of our baby girl more than made up for it for the both of us. God was so good and was still blessing.

KEN: I didn't want to leave Alison and Ellie in the hospital but at such short notice there was no choice but for me to go and be at my station in Dublin. It was the official evening of my ordination in Whitewell and all the wheels were set in motion with visitors coming to the event. There was a coach load coming from Dublin and my family were going to be there so things had to go on at this point. I thought I'd get a quick chance to call in to see Alison, Jodie and our new baby Ellie on the way home but this meant the coach coming along with me.

When we pulled up to the house I could see Alison through the window looking out at me and some of the coach-load of people who were starting to disembark to come in to see the new arrival, she was what looked like morphing before my eyes, from disbelief to embarrassment to confusion to I'm going to kill him!

The ordination...

The ordination was held in Whitewell under the leadership of their senior Pastor, James McConnell. Setting me apart for ministry by the laying on of hands and prayer before God and the church for a witness as the pastor of the church in Dublin. I was already there under some training and supervision but now I was being sent on my own.

It was an amazing night. After Pastor McConnell had preached a powerful gospel message he called me and all the pastors and elders of the church up onto the platform. I got on my knees and surrounded by the leaders of God's church, Pastor McConnell suddenly stopped and called for oil to anoint me.

He anointed me with oil and prayed over me to set me aside for the work of the Lord but then he also prayed a prophetic office over my life and ministry.

What an amazing time we were having in the presence of the Saviour as we sang and worshipped. The Spirit of God came among us and I was aware that He rested upon me. I received that night and still hold to that fact that a ministry of impartation happened as from then on I knew and saw a difference in my ministry.

ALISON: Obviously I wasn't there for Ken's ordination but I remember a real change in him from that night. Even though Ken had already been baptised in the Spirit, from that night it seemed to be amplified. It wasn't an immediate change but over a period of time, the Lord was increasing Ken's gifts.

The one thing about Dublin was, it felt like he had a much more spiritual liberty. People there were a lot more open to the gifts and the baptism and moving of the Holy Spirit. It was in Dublin that Ken learned how to use his gifts.

Yes, that's right. I remember we had a mission in Dublin and we were having times of prayer beforehand. One Tuesday night when we met for the prayer meeting, we were in the main part of the church. There was a good crowd that night. We were worshipping and praying about the upcoming two-week mission. As we were singing, I started to feel like oil was dripping from my hands and they were warm. I remember the strong anointing that came over me at this point. As I was standing there, the Lord said to me; "All who will take part – go and lay hands on them and pray."

So everybody was just praising in their rows of seats, I walked along and as I lay hands on them, only just touching them, the people were bursting into ecstatic praise. Some were shouting and praising, others crying and weeping. The anointing was strong, it was like a fire had ignited the people. Some were speaking in tongues. As this was happening, the room just continued to fill.

There was a friend of mine, who had been travelling down with me occasionally, he was in the meeting that night and he was from a Presbyterian background. He wasn't used to anything spiritual or Pentecostal in nature. He was standing at his seat and he had his eyes closed, he was praying. He knew something was happening but he didn't know what was going on. I prayed with the person in front of him who was going to be serving at the mission. I didn't know this until later, when I laid hands on them they felt the same way. They told me it was like somebody had set fire to them.

He became affected too, he told me afterwards that he felt physically weak, like he couldn't stand. When we were leaving to go home, he was sitting in the car and he was exhausted. He said to me; "Now I know the reality of the power of God." I asked him why that was? He said; "You were praying for a person in front of me and when you were praying for them, I could hardly stand. I didn't know what was happening. I just felt it moving from where you were with that man over me. It was like something had washed over me."

And from that night, he changed his mind about the things of the spirit and it became real to him. The things of the Holy Ghost became part of his everyday seeking and experience.

We then continued on and had our two-week mission held in the heart of Dublin in St. Stephen's Green. There were 46 people saved during the mission, back then that was amazing as the Dublin people were very hard. On the last night we had a healing service.

Throughout the mission there was a particular young woman who loved what we were doing and it was very clear the Lord had caught hold of her. She was a Christian and actually aired a weekly slot on a local radio station on a Sunday, talking about the Lord.

After the service, she asked me if I would go on the radio to preach the gospel. So I agreed and started making pre-recordings in Whitewell and then she would play them on her show every Sunday. It was a great outlet, it also gave me an opportunity to preach in Tallaght as that was where she was from.

At the healing service on the last night, a young man came with leukaemia. He had been recently given six months to live, giving him at this point only three months left. We prayed with him and he is still alive. There were real miraculous times in Dublin but it was a hard place to minister.

Even with the miraculous comes the other side that no one likes to see. On my first official week in Dublin, one of the ladies who attended the church, her husband tragically hung himself. It was certainly a baptism of fire for me but we rallied around the family and tried to do our best. With her husband dead, the house was falling into disrepair so I got a few guys together and the next weekend we drove down to Dublin and we painted the house for them.

I remember we were painting away and my mate Gary disappeared, I went to see what had happened him as I could hear shouting from another room. I walked in and found Patricia's three boys and a room-full of their friends sitting in front of the TV watching the football. They were huge Celtic fans and the match was Celtic vs Rangers. They were yelling at the TV wearing their green striped tops, of course stuck in the middle of it was Gary – a huge Rangers fan! The sweat broke on me, I thought; "Is he trying to get us killed?"

I said to them; "Right boys, if Rangers win this match then you have to come to church on Sunday!" They weren't buying it at all but I told them that if they were confident in their team then they had nothing to worry about! I left Gary and them watching the match, I figured he could hold his own.

Unfortunately Celtic won that day but later on the boys did come to church with their mum and they really took an interest. They all made professions and I had the pleasure of baptising them.

We hired a pool and I was standing in the water and these three teenage boys came out to get baptised wearing their Celtic tops. So when they were standing with me I said to them; "Guys, I have already taught you about baptism, you understand what you are doing, what it means." They agreed. I continued about dying to self in the waters of baptism and rising to life in Christ and they nodded. They were very serious. So I tried to inject a little humour. I said to them; "Now do you see these Celtic tops?" Yes they said. "Do you realise that when I baptise you, when you come up they will be Rangers ones?"

We all laughed, I had a great rapport with them, it was good fun. It was great to see such a change in them after the tragic circumstances when we first met.

A hard calling...

We had some great times in Dublin, some fun times but it was hard going. It was a hard slog for us. Part of the problem we had was the driving up and down, this was before they had the motorway completed. We were driving from Belfast to Dublin with a toddler and a newborn at that time and that's a long time in the car. It wasn't very pleasant. We were leaving Belfast at 7.30am and I was driving along trying to prepare for the meeting ahead and trying to switch off the noise inside the car of a bored child and a baby crying. Having to push ahead in case we had to make stops for potty training etc. It certainly took its toll.

When we arrived in Dublin, we had to clean the building and set it up before everyone arrived. I preached, I played the guitar for the worship, I did everything at the meeting and Alison took care of all the children, it was hard work.

Dublin was difficult for our relationship as I really loved to be with Alison and that just wasn't possible. When I was preaching and ministering, she was stuck out back in a small room with the children. I felt so detached from her as I always felt God had called us to minister as a couple. I tried asking for more help in the crèche but nobody volunteered.

Things have been difficult for the girls too through everything as we have had a lot of moves and upheaval. They had to travel where we were going, the long journeys up and down to Dublin were taxing on them.

We persevered for almost three years and when the opportunity wasn't opening to acquire a house closer to the church, we took it as a sign to start to seek God's will on the issue. We were fully convinced that it was time to leave but only after a lot of searching and God's confirmation.

ALISON: I was just happy supporting Ken. I know some people/ pastors would have it as Pastor Davidson and Pastor Alison, but to me that's two different pastors with two different roles and I just don't see it like that. That's two people jockeying, that's two careers so to me that can pull a marriage apart. So, I see it as, I support Ken in his ministry and my job is to be his support, to be his back-up. I believe I am called to be Ken's help-meet, I am to support him, hold his hands up if he is weary but never to usurp his authority. He is the priest and the head of our home. I believe that is the biblical principal set out in the Bible.

Especially when we were in Dublin, the madness that went on meant that there was just a continual, constant need for Ken. So when he came home my idea was that he should be able to leave that stress behind and come into a calm environment. I don't believe you should be clashing with each other, but rather supporting each other, lifting each other up. In essence – that is ministry.

By looking after me, Alison was ministering to me. I have been really blessed with Alison. I think it would be very difficult for a pastor to minister without having a godly wife behind him. To me it would be nearly impossible to be the best I can be without that support at home. When I came home, Alison was always there as a tower of strength especially at times when I could have collapsed under the weight of the stress. She is the one who has held me up, mentally helping me. Obviously the Lord is our strength but she has been the one who has been beside me, behind me and supported me.

In Romania especially, when we had nobody – we had each other. One person I am able to trust is my wife. And it's off that strength comes, one can chase 1,000 and two can chase 10,000. (Deuteronomy 32:30) It's that unity, it's that bond. Two become one flesh but we are also one spirit in the Lord. With all of that, we have found that is where our strength is. No matter what comes our way, yes we have had times where we have disagreed or bounced off each other but in the end of it, we are one. We are together in this. That is something that has brought us through a lot.

Section 8

When the path gets steep – keep going!

'We are troubled on every side, yet not distressed;
we are perplexed, but not in despair; Persecuted,
but not forsaken; cast down, but not destroyed;
Always bearing about in the body the dying of the
Lord Jesus, that the life also of Jesus might be made
manifest in our body. For we which live are always
delivered unto death for Jesus' sake, that the life also
of Jesus might be made manifest in our mortal flesh.'

2 Corinthians 4:8-11

Chapter Eighteen
Developing a Godly Christian relationship...

At the start of our relationship, I would have been very quick to tell Alison when I wasn't happy about something. I know looking back, I would have been quite aggressive in my mannerisms and that just didn't work. Alison was very patient with me in those first few years of marriage. I can see now that I didn't value her, I thought I did but really I didn't. I will include her in all my decisions now which before I wouldn't have, I didn't run things past her at all. Now it is more of a partnership and we work really well together.

Trust is a very important component in a successful marriage. We trust each other completely and are transparent with each other. I gave Alison all my passwords for my email accounts/social media etc. This means that I am not hiding anything from my wife and I am not opening myself up to anything being misinterpreted.

Being conscious of the Lord is the main gel for making any partnership work. He is the centre of everything that we do. Our life revolves around ministry, it's both of us in it, sharing the things of ministry together. We are conscious that everything we say to each other and everything we do is in front of the Lord as He is the head. What I think helps us as well, I am very easy-going and Alison is easily pleased – its a great combination!

ALISON: Ken is the head of the home but I am the neck that turns it and that neck is not as stiff to turn as it was! He is my best friend, my support and he is the person that I would talk things over with. We are constantly talking. Good communication is vital for a marriage to succeed. Even though you can be together physically as a couple, having quality time together is essential.

We make a point every week to have some time for just the both of us. Even though we are together every day, we never get tired of each other's company.

As a pastor's wife you do become very protective of your marriage. I am aware that we have a good marriage and I know that the enemy's tactics would be to target it. Marriage has been a lot of pastors' undoing so it is something that I would watch out for.

The Lord is the cord in our marriage, He keeps us strong together, as the Word says; *'A threefold cord is not quickly broken.'* Ecclesiastes 4:9.

I have my own walk and calling in the Lord which compliments Ken's ministry and his mine as we minister together. I am the one who comes alongside him and strengthens his hand. Ken is the head of the home but he must submit unto God. Ken is the head of me but I must submit unto Ken. I couldn't do that if I didn't trust him completely. True submission is what is lacking now in marriages and it plays a huge role in the breakdown of relationships. Wives are becoming so dominant now in the marriage that men are afraid to be men any more. How many Godly men do you see in today's society who are priests in their own home? It is so rare now.

My role is to compliment Ken, and walk beside him.

The perseverance of the saints...

In 2 Corinthians 4:8-11, it says; *'We are troubled on every side, yet not distressed; we are perplexed, but not in despair; Persecuted, but not forsaken; cast down, but not destroyed; Always bearing about in the body the dying of the Lord Jesus, that the life also of Jesus might be made manifest in our body. For we which live are always delivered unto death for Jesus' sake, that the life also of Jesus might be made manifest in our mortal flesh.'*

In today's church, you would rarely hear from many pulpits, words like troubled, perplexed, persecuted and cast down. The modern theme today by many is that when you come to Christ, all is rosy and all is great but that's not the gospel at all. The apostle Paul tells of his own life how he endured all these things. Now the cry may be; "Hide those words Paul, let's skip 2 Corinthians 4 and let's move onto something nicer in case it puts people off coming to Christ." But when you take the teachings of the Lord, Jesus Christ, He never once tried to fool people that it was going to be easy.

He didn't give them a false ideology that it was all going to be plain sailing. In fact, He told the people that they *would* have persecution in this world but He said; *'Ye shall have tribulation: but be of good cheer; I have overcome the world.'* John 16:33.

We must expand and expound these things as if we were honest before God, we would all say; "I agree, it happens to me."

It's not the trouble or the persecution but rather it's Paul's example of perseverance in it and through it. That's what Paul is telling us here, he isn't saying God is going to lift you up out of it and drop you somewhere else. It's the persevering through it. Sometimes your trials can be for a short time but the Christian life is a complete perseverance. When you walk faithfully, you will encounter those that will rise up against you. People are going to disagree with you and some will not want to hear the gospel or walk in righteousness. Sometimes our opposition can come from other

Christians who feel that they are more superior than us, spiritually higher than us.

Paul isn't saying here about who is higher than anyone else, he is saying – watch how we persevere, watch where our strength comes from, watch where our hope is. Paul is saying this even as an apostle of the Lord Jesus Christ. Notice what he says here, he says it is not you and I who are thinking; "Well, we will pray and everything will be over, if it isn't over then God's not answering." He is saying, there is perseverance through it and he wants us to see the example of the perseverance of the saints. It's about Paul's trial and Paul's testings. It's about his weaknesses, of those I have plenty.

We all have weaknesses, Paul was no exception but it is about God's strength in him.

It's about Paul overcoming all these things, trouble, perplexity, being cast down. It's him coming through it with the inestimable love of God and the sovereign grace that keeps him going on. Paul shows this example to illustrate that the centre isn't Paul because he is the one being persecuted. He is not the centre. The persecutions that are coming from every direction are not the centre.

When you and I start to feel these troubles and persecutions, we either become the centre which means we are no good to anyone else or else they become our centre and that's all we can see. That's all we know, that's all we can accept. Paul is not saying he is the centre, he's saying the troubles aren't the centre but rather he points us to Christ. And he says; 'He is in the centre of it all.' It is His glorification that we look for in everything we face in life. The perseverance of the saints is a manifest life of the working of the Holy Ghost. It's the sovereign grace of God in you and you carrying on, even through your failures. Even through all your faults. Even when we are persecuted, when we are weak. When we feel like we can't go on, God perseveres in you and through you. When we get to the end of that trial or problem, when we get to the end of whatever has rose against us, whether it be in our body, mind, home, workplace, from our neighbours, whatever angle it comes from. Scripture states in Ephesians 6; *'...having done all, to stand. Stand...'* (13-14) We can think it is us that is holding us – look at me, I got through this, see how strong I am. Really, the revelation is, seeing how weak I am, I couldn't have got through it without Him. Paul is saying here, centralise yourself. Focus your heart, your all, on Christ. He is your strength. He is your focus. This perseverance is the outworking of the Holy Ghost in your life, in your walk with Christ. He is giving you experience. With perseverance comes patience which is a hard thing to learn. I have to admit, sometimes I have no patience, it certainly doesn't come naturally to me. I want it yesterday, I want it happened, I want it done. I get frustrated with things that are not done quickly. Tribulation worketh patience and patience, experience.

Experience can give hope. Hope that makes you not ashamed. So from your tribulation to your hope that makes you not ashamed, Christ was there all the time. He was leading you, breaking you, moulding you, bringing you right through all of it.

Some of you reading this are at the tribulation end, some of you are in a certain circumstance at the patience end. Some of you are experiencing what really happens in your walk with Christ. Some have come through a certain storm and you have realised that you are at hope because Christ has been there the whole time. It's that hope that makes you not ashamed.

I remember the old song we used to sing; *'Standing somewhere in the shadows, you'll find Jesus.'* In many of our lives, we look for Him and we can't find Him because He just doesn't seem as vibrant as He was before. He seems to be a little bit further away than He was before this happened because you think He has moved. But here is the thing – He said; *'I will never leave thee, nor forsake thee.'* Hebrews 13:5. So whatever way you look at it, He can't move, He can't leave you because He has promised and His promises are, 'Yes and Amen.' (2 Corinthians 1:20) You are His and sealed in Him with love.

It's not *if*, but *when* we go through these dark seasons, we realise that in the perseverance of His people, He keeps us through *'the power of God through faith unto salvation.'* 1 Peter 1:5. It is God working through us.

Notice how Paul wrote in 2 Corinthians 4:8; *'We are troubled on every side, yet not distressed.'* He wrote *'we are perplexed but not in despair.'* *'We are persecuted but not forsaken.'* *'We are cast down but not destroyed.'*

You may be troubled but if you allow God's Word to enter into your heart and your mind, into your situation, you will find that you will not be in despair. Inside you somewhere, there's a still small voice that tells you; "Look, I've got this. I'm still on the throne."

We say; "But Lord I see all this, all around me." He replies; "Yes ,but that's not the centre." We say; "But Lord, what about me?" But you see – you're not the centre. He says; "I have it, I have it all under control. No matter what comes against you. I am still in charge."

So you aren't in despair. Then secondly, perplexed. Being perplexed simply means, you don't know whether you are coming or going. Things are just against you. I have personally experienced this, where I just wanted to jump out of my body, leave my skin and be somewhere else. I have been perplexed many times. It happens when we focus on ourselves. "What am I going to do?" "How am I going to fix this?" You are inwardly looking, you are looking on self and it just doesn't work.

I recall one of my congregation said to me; "Pastor, I have been praying about it but it's out of my hands."

I said; "Good, because you are making a mess of it. It's in God's hands, leave it there."

The best place for your problems to be, is in God's hands. The longer you hold onto these things, the heavier they get. The longer you grasp it and refuse to let go of the problem or situation, thinking you can change something that can't be changed, then the harder it is going to be for you to carry it.

The Lord has had to tell me off a few times but I remember one time in particular, I was praying about my ministry at the time, I prayed; "Lord, do you see this church, they are putting my head away! Please help. I am at my wits end here, I can't cope!" I was walking along crying out to God; "Lord where are you? Help me."

All I could hear was this still, small voice saying; "I never told you to carry it anyway. It's not your church, it's mine."

Obviously I already knew that, but the realisation that came when the Word entered my heart was overwhelming. It just lifted it all from me because it was the truth and it set me free. Persecuted but not forsaken. Who is against you? I have had many people come against me in my life. What do we do when people rise against us? It's not nice but we can't go into a wee corner and hide, we need to stand firm and say to the Lord; "Lord, sort this out, it's up to you." We may be at the end of our rope, but with Christ we are never at the end of our hope!

You may feel you're at the end of your rope, and the problem lies with many people feeling they can't go on, but with Christ you're never at the end of your hope.

Take that and say; "Lord we are not forsaken, you've never left us, we are cast down but not destroyed." It's natural to become cast down through circumstance, but when you do, just get back up again, get up again and go on with God.

When I was in my 20's, I had many fights in the ring. I remember when I was sitting in the changing rooms, getting ready beforehand, a cold sweat used to break on me. My nerves heightened, as the adrenalin built. Outside, I could hear the crowds cheering, it felt like I was going out into a Roman coliseum. As I walked out, my legs were shaking with nerves. However, when you get up those steps and in through the ropes, as you do, you start thinking differently.

It's time to step up, you're nervous, even fear can grip you, but here's the thing, its not the size of the dog in the fight, it's the size of the fight in the dog! If you're a Christian, the fight in you is Almighty God. I remember when the referee dropped his hand for round one, the fear left me instantly because the job in hand came clearly into view.

I remember when I was fighting for the British title in Manchester, I was so tired coming to the last round of the fight, that I felt my whole lower half leaving me. It was just sheer exhaustion. And I remember feeling like I was going down. I could feel my legs going from below me, sinking lower and lower and at the last second 'ding ding.' I was saved by the bell. I was never as glad to hear the bell ringing. I was defeated on points that time.

There are times we feel we are captured, our legs are buckling as our spiritual weakness is so great, we feel we are never going to make it to the end, then suddenly the bell rings, you're not destroyed. Son/daughter here is your way of escape, Jesus has come to save. He comes into the situation. Sometimes when you're in the midst of the fight, a three-minute round seems like a three-hour round! Our perishable bodies are subject to sin and suffering, but God has never abandoned us because Christ has given you and I the Word of authority to be victorious over it all. Remember Jesus paid for all our sins, past, present and future but he also paid for my sicknesses. He has given us the authority and ability.

Paul's thorn in the flesh is not a literal thorn, it's not a sickness either, this is people. Paul is worn down with persecution of people, do you realise the more God reveals to you, the more the enemy hates you for it and wants to see you persecuted and cast down. That's why we need to praise and glorify Christ and believe God for bigger things again, every step you take.

The more God gives you, the more your metal will be tested, your faith will be tested. Have you ever heard the Scripture; *'My grace is sufficient for thee,'* have you read the rest of the verse? *'My grace is sufficient for thee'?* Paul actually writes, *'My grace is sufficient for thee: for my strength is made perfect in weakness. Most gladly therefore will I rather glory in my infirmities, that the power of Christ may rest upon me.'* 2 Corinthians 12:9.

Paul was saying, if it takes this to have more of Christ, then I'm willing to go through it, I don't want this but if this is what it takes, so be it, I will still praise you, I will still love you, I will still follow you, I will still serve you, I will still go on with you, I will still trust, hope and be with you, as long as I have Christ. Far too many Christians faint too easily, they fall at the slightest temptation, they are too easily offended, they are easily put off their service to Christ. They are too easy to lose heart in their trials and they walk away from the Lord.

On 29th October 1941, Winston Churchill gave a speech at Harrow School. He got up in front of all the pupils and this was his speech; "Never give in. Never give in. Never, never, never, never — in nothing, great or small, large or petty — never give in, except to convictions of honour and good sense." On a different occasion he said; "The pessimist sees the problems in every opportunity, whereas the optimist always sees the opportunity in every problem."

You should be looking at your problem without seeing the problem itself, you should be seeing the opportunity to do something and to show the glory of Christ in it.

Someone once wrote; "The number one reason why people give up so fast is that they tend to look at how far they have to go, rather than how far they have already gotten."

You've come further than you have yet to go!

Chapter Nineteen
Mountain-top experience in Carnmoney...

After Dublin I stopped preaching for 10 months, I cancelled all my dates. I was given a secular job in Carrickfergus so to avoid the travel, we moved to Carnmoney. A friend of mine was a director of a local company and he made a job for me to help us out. I had no idea what I was doing but it gave us a little security again and we concentrated on building our family. At that time Ellie in particular had no bond with me as I hadn't been at home, so this was my time to start building relationships with the girls.

We went back to attending Whitewell. I wanted to concentrate on my family but I also needed a break. In Dublin, I was giving out the whole time, so I was exhausted. During our time in Carnmoney, it wasn't that I had given up on the Lord but I was just looking for the path out of this season. I was looking for where God would lead me to. I felt that I had been so busy, now, I needed to step back and wait on Him. There was one point where I even felt that I didn't want to preach again. At that time, I remember being so miserable. It was just awful.

ALISON: He was as miserable as sin and I was having a great time! I loved our time in Carnmoney as Ken worked a normal job, he had a half-day on a Friday so we had the whole weekend to ourselves. On Sunday we went to church together as a family and were able to sit together which never happened before. Before Ken was always up at the pulpit and I was sitting on my own trying to keep two children quiet. I was just the constant childminder but now we were in church as a family and I really enjoyed it.

For me, the Lord had just placed us on this little mountain, in a quiet cul de sac, it was so peaceful just for us to have quality, family time. We no longer had the hassles and pressures of being a pastor and a pastor's wife, the phone wasn't ringing throughout the night or Ken having to leave the dinner table just as he had sat down.

Some men preach to live but I live to preach! I just can't help it. The rest in Carnmoney was much needed and it was enjoyable but it didn't last long, I was missing preaching. God had placed this desire in me, He had given it to me. I tried to reject what God had for me, even to the point where I was saying that I just wasn't doing it any more. It is like when Jeremiah said; *'His word was in mine heart as a burning fire shut up in my bones.'* Jeremiah 20:9.

I just couldn't hold it any more, I had to give it out or I thought I would blow up!

Days later, Alison said; "Ken, as happy as we are here, you are not happy within yourself." And she was right, I was content in many ways but I was struggling as I knew I wasn't doing what the Lord wanted me to do. However, this time I wanted to do things differently as what this experience taught me was... Yes, I had been obedient in Dublin but I had been doing God's work at the expense of my wife and children. I realised then, God wouldn't want me to do that.

I really felt I had to take that step back and learn how to prioritise my life as a husband and father. It is Christ first, then my wife and children, then church and ministry. It was getting it into the right order that really changed my life and life took on a whole new meaning with ministry following.

Dear reader, don't risk trying to save the world by losing your family. When I got these things in the right order then the Lord blessed us.

A divine encounter?...

I really started to feel that the Lord was giving me a fresh direction but I didn't know what to or where to. One day I drove the car to the garage to have it washed. As I was driving, instead of going to the local garage, I ended up driving six miles to Belfast. I don't know why, but I just kept on driving.

I pulled into a garage on the Shankill Road and could see the lance wash was free but there was a car parked in front of it, I pulled in behind it to see if they were going to use the wash. The car didn't move so I parked over in a space. It was a token wash so I had to go into the garage to get a token to use it.

As I was walking back out from the shop, the man who was in the car in front was walking towards me. We looked at each other and nodded as if we knew each other. My phone rang, I took the call, it was my brother. So, I was standing talking to him on the phone, token in my hand when I noticed this same man coming back from the garage, walking towards me again. I watched as he got into his car, as he did I felt the Lord say to me; "Hang up and go and speak to him." So I told Stephen that I would speak to him later, I hung up the call and walked over to the man. I hadn't a clue what I was going to say.

I got his attention then I just said; "Excuse me, do I know you?"

He said; "I don't know but I thought I knew you."

We then tried to figure out where we could know each other from. Then it dawned on me, he was an Elim pastor.

He told me that he was retiring, then he said to me; "Aren't you Ken Davidson who went to Dublin for Whitewell?" I confirmed that I was.

He asked me; "What are you doing now?" I told him I was currently in secular work. He looked shocked and asked me why I was doing that?

I told him that I just wanted a break after Dublin to see where the Lord was leading me. We had a good chat about the Lord's work and he asked me to come and preach for him in Cullybackey. I agreed and gave him my details, he was to ring me with a date when he got home. Then he said to me; "Why don't you give the Superintendent, Eric McComb a ring and see if anything happens from that?"

I said; "No, because I am not kicking any doors open by myself, if that's what God has for me, Eric will ring me." He laughed and warned me that Eric was a very busy man and hard to get, he didn't believe he would contact me but I didn't mind, I wasn't ringing him.

It was a bizarre meeting; the pastor had told me that he had been driving up the M2 and the Lord had told him to turn and go back. He hadn't a clue how he ended up in that garage but he parked in front of the wash and asked the Lord; "Lord why am I here?" That was just before I pulled in behind him. I told him then that I was going to wash my car in the local garage and ended up driving into Belfast instead. He said to me; "Surely this is of the Lord."

I said; "Yes, it looks like it but I am still not calling Eric McComb."

We said our goodbyes and headed our separate ways.

About four weeks later, it was a Monday morning and our phone rang, Alison answered it. It was Eric McComb wanting to speak to me. Alison came and got me, she was really startled-looking as obviously I had told her that if I didn't contact Eric, he wouldn't contact me but now he was on the telephone. I took the call and he said; "My name is Eric McComb, I don't know if it means anything to you?"

I said; "Yes, it does. I know who you are."

He continued; "I have heard about you, I was given your number on a piece of paper. Actually I have quite a few numbers of pieces of paper in my pocket but most times I just throw them out but I felt strongly of the Lord to phone this one, this morning."

I said; "Okay." I wasn't really sure what to say.

Then he said; "Do you want to come and meet with me for a chat?" So I agreed.

Out of that chat, we agreed that I would preach in several Elim churches until we would both see how the Lord was directing.

At the next meeting I had with Eric, we were discussing what church opportunities there were and towards the end he looked at me and said; "What do you want?"

I said; "I want what God wants."

He sighed and said; "I have nothing left to offer you."

So I said to him; "That's okay, God mustn't have anything here for me then."

And then he said; "We only have..." then he paused. "No, we are going to close that."

I said; "Where is that?"

He said; "No it doesn't matter, the decision has been made to close it."

I enquired again, where it was.

He said; "Donaghcloney." As soon as he said it, I just knew, I had to go there! I knew by the look on his face, he was thinking; "This man is nuts!"

The reason I knew this was for me, was because a few years earlier when we were living in Donaghcloney and I had ill health, I was out walking one morning and I stopped outside the church. As I did, I felt the Lord telling me that I was going to be in there, that He was going to place me there. I dismissed it, I definitely thought I was hearing things! But here I was now being given an opportunity to go to that very church. Eric told me that he would organise it so I could go firstly and preach there but he told me that there were very few in attendance.

A move in faith...

When I went to preach in Donaghcloney Elim for the first time, there were eight people there in total. The congregation was run down and the church was in debt so the decision was taken to close it. As it was so poorly attended, there was no way they could offer me a full-time wage if I was to take the post. If this was for me, then I would have to go in faith. I knew this is what the Lord had for us so I said that I would go.

The first Sunday morning we were there, the church building was near empty, as only fourteen of us were in attendance, that was including our family and two of our friends. Afterwards we went to Alison's parents' house and I went into their back room and got on my knees.

I came before the Lord and said; "Are you sure about this Lord because I am not!"

"Have you seen this place?"

Alison's dad was saying to me afterwards; "I don't know why you chose that church to come to, its dying on its feet! There are already five churches in Donaghcloney, where do you think the people are going to come from?"

Things weren't looking good but yet I still felt I was meant to be there.

So we went back that night and there were a couple of new people there but still a very poor turnout.

The congregation began to grow and yet as it was growing, people were dying. In the first year that I was there, I buried fifteen people from the congregation. I soon learned that the turnout was poor as the congregation was an older one so they were no longer fit or able to attend. I spent a lot of my time visiting them at their homes and in the nursing home.

As the members were all of an elder age, we decided to try and encourage a younger generation, so we planned a children's meeting.

I went one day around the doors in the village with Jodie and Ellie, inviting people to come along. The children's meeting took off, it went really well. We gathered around 40 children from the village and they all had a great time.

We then started to have missions, people were getting saved, things were starting to grow. We started to develop a presence among the people, out walking around and meeting them at school times, developing relationships. We ran community fun days that got people used to coming inside the church building. This then grew into a youth ministry and a ladies fellowship. We did everything ourselves, from cleaning the church to ministering, we literally had to put our hands to the plough and do it all.

The Lord kept giving the increase, things were blossoming and growing.

In 2012, we felt led to do a tent mission. It was our most ambitious plan to date. We planned a 'big tent event' with no money as the church was still in debt... faith was stirring! We asked the local school if they would lend us their gravel pitches to use for the tents and they agreed. We got a 1,000-seater tent, we didn't realise how big that would be. It nearly took up the entire school grounds. It was that big, it even had its own kitchen. We borrowed chairs from schools all around the local area. We gave out 20,000 leaflets, advertised it on the radio and got huge banners printed. We also had it printed on the side of a minibus and I drove it to a local popular shopping centre and parked it. It was all go!

Friday night was the youth night, we had a youth band playing, a Northern Ireland evangelist and football player, Stuart Elliott preached the Word and the Ulster Rugby player, Paul Marshall, came and shared his testimony at it. On the Friday night we were amazed that around 400 people attended.

On the Saturday we had a fun day. There was an army and police vehicle show, stunt bikes, pony rides, go-karting, archery, birds of prey, a puppet show, face painting, balloons, goody bags. It was very popular and successful. Everything was free for those attending, all just to bless the local community of which several thousand attended. We had the opportunity to witness to many about the love of Christ.

That evening, I preached about lost things from Luke 15. There were about 600 people in attendance. There were testimonies shared and at the end of the service, several people gave their lives to Christ.

Sunday night we decided just to have our own church service in the tent, the plan being afterwards, we would have a second meeting for everyone to attend for worship and healing. This would allow everyone to attend their own churches first. So we began our service with just our own people, there were about sixty of us in total, the tent looked really empty but we carried on. As the service started, the people kept arriving and at the end of the night, every chair was filled! Some people stayed on for the healing service but some left, however those that left, their seats were quickly filled by new people arriving. It was just amazing. People were getting saved and others were receiving healing.

There were many amazing healings taking place. I remember this one woman that came for prayer. She had an irregular heartbeat and the doctors couldn't do anything for her. She had been given a pacemaker but it was still causing her problems. As we were praying for her, there was a lady from our church that had the same problem. She was standing worshipping two rows back and as we prayed for this woman, the two of them were healed at the same time!

During the meeting earlier, a man had become born-again and he stayed after the service for prayer. The following Sunday when he arrived at church he told me to look at his hands. I didn't understand, but he told me that his hands were curled like claws and were full of psoriasis. His hands were now straightened and his skin was as soft as a baby's, he was delighted.

There was a girl came who had 26 serious asthma attacks that year, she was prayed for and has never had one since. Her brother had an in-turned foot, he was due an operation to break his leg in order to correct it. We prayed and he never had to have the operation, he is still well today.

One of our neighbours came who had a degenerative heart condition, when she returned to her specialist she was told that her degenerative condition had ceased. It was a miracle, the specialist said that it is called degenerative as it continues to get worse, it cannot stop but her's had. No matter what denomination or communities, God was reaching people.

We were amazed at what the Lord was doing. It took us to be obedient to the Lord. Going to that small church was a huge leap of faith for us, but to see how the Lord was moving among the people was so rewarding.

Chapter Twenty
A Season of Death...

Just as things were improving for us in our church life, unfortunately, our family life was going into a state of crisis.

Ken's eldest sister, Elaine, who was only 46, was taken into a nursing home. This was a real shock to everyone as she was so young compared to the other patients. She had severe diabetes which left her with lots of pains in her body and her sight was really bad. Her kidney function was very poor and she needed dialysis, they just couldn't work with her any more at her house so unfortunately the move was necessary for her to receive the care she needed. She was very ill, it was very distressing for the entire family to see her in such a state.

During this time, we would have made a point of going to visit her every Friday night and Saturday. We dropped the girls off with Grandad Ken and then went on to see Elaine. For the first while she was in the home, because she was getting the quality of nursing she needed and they were keeping her diet right, she really began to blossom. They cared for her much better than we could have. Things were going really well but it was in late November, when her health started to decline. She wasn't really out of bed and if she was, it was only for very short periods of time, then back in bed.

Her dialysis had stopped working and her kidneys were shutting down. She was too ill to have a transplant, so things were looking very bleak. We explored all the options, looking at any matches in the family but the doctors advised that it wouldn't be successful.

At this time, we also noticed that things weren't good with Ken's other sister, Heather. We noticed she wasn't visiting Grandad Ken. Before, when we would have left the girls with him, Heather would have called round to see them, but she just stopped coming so we were concerned. We then found out that her husband, William had been diagnosed with a brain tumour. The doctors told him that he would probably only survive a couple of years. He was in his mid-forties, it was just an awful blow to the family, especially with Elaine being so ill. Knowing about William, we understood Heather was under pressure at home. She was also worried about her sister but little did we know that Heather was actually ill too.

KEN: Things were really hard in the family, I was worried about the strain everyone was under, it was taking its toll on my dad. Heather was really starting to disappear and he was missing having her about.

One weekend in late November when we arrived to see Elaine, we knew things weren't good, she was very low. Alison was trying to get her more comfortable in the bed, plumping her pillows and rubbing her back, but she looked very weak. I rested on the side of her bed and she reached out to me and tried to pull me close, I leaned over to her and she was saying something to me but as her voice was so weak I couldn't understand her. She said something again and then she fell into a deep sleep. Alison and I decided to go and let her rest, we could see she was starting to sleep a lot more.

On the Sunday night, I was just going out the door to church when the phone rang, I lifted the phone and it was my dad. I thought something had happened to Elaine but he was actually ringing about Heather. He told me that she hadn't been very well at all, that's why she hadn't been around much. I was shocked to learn this, I assumed it had been because of William being ill.

I asked him what was wrong with her?

He said; "She has been taken into hospital." I was dumbfounded, I asked him what had happened and he said that he didn't really know but they thought it was something to do with her liver. He told me that the ambulance had to get her. I told him that I was on my way out to take a meeting but as soon as it was over, I would go straight down to the hospital. At that time I had no idea how serious her condition was otherwise I would have went straight to the hospital. I went to the meeting and preached, I got someone else to close the meeting and Alison and I got into the car and drove to Belfast.

I just couldn't understand how Heather could be ill. When we arrived at the Royal, we found Heather and she was extremely jaundiced, even her eyeballs were yellow. She had lines in her arms and she seemed very confused.

We sat trying to talk to her for a little while and she started to come around, talking more sense. She began to be more coherent, obviously the treatment she was receiving was starting to take effect. The doctor spoke to us and said that she was very ill and it could take four weeks before she would be fit to go home. At this point it was late, about 11pm so we said goodnight to her and we called in to check on my dad, just to make sure he was okay.

On the way to Dad's I remember saying to Alison that I wasn't happy about Elaine, I just wanted to see her. I had a really bad feeling about her, that something was wrong. Alison told me to go and see her if I wanted even though it was late. I didn't know what to do so I decided that I would leave it until the morning as I had told Heather that I would visit her, so I could call with them both then.

I struggled to sleep as I just had so much in my head with my sisters now both being so ill. I lay in bed praying for a little while and eventually fell asleep. I was wakened by the phone ringing, Alison answered it, it was my dad. I knew something was seriously wrong.

The phone rang in the middle of the night, I lifted it quickly so it wouldn't waken the girls. When I heard it was Ken's dad, I knew it was bad news.

He said to me; "She's dead!" I thought he meant Heather, the hospital must have rang.

I then said; "Who is dead, Dad?"

He said; "Elaine is dead, the home just rang." I was so shocked.

Ken could overhear our conversation and he went into shock.

We got out of bed and went down to the home, they had been working with her but she was dead. She had simply slipped away in her sleep, the nursing staff had checked on her but knew she was gone.

Her daughter Stacy was there, her husband Thomas and Ken's dad. As we sat in the nursing home, we were very concerned about Stacy, and Elaine's son, Jack. They had just lost their mother and it was very unexpected. Later we discussed Heather, should we tell her what's happened? With her being so ill we didn't want to set her back. So we decided to keep it quiet so she could recover. The family all looked to Ken, as he was a pastor they all wanted him to direct operations. We organised everyone so that there was always family calling with Heather during visiting times while others organised Elaine's funeral. It was really stressful.

Elaine was buried on the Thursday. The funeral went smoothly but it was awful without Heather.

KEN: The funeral was very hard, I couldn't believe she was gone. After the burial, Heather's husband, William came over to me and whispered to me; "Ken, you need to get your Dad down home, I just got a call from the hospital and Heather is very ill, she has taken a turn for the worse."

I got Dad in the car and didn't tell him why we were leaving sharply. We drove him to his home to call the hospital, we then told him what was happening. When we arrived at the hospital, my Dad went inside with Alanah, Heather's daughter and we waited outside as there was only two allowed in per bed.

After a short while, my dad reappeared with his arms around Alanah, he looked at me and shook his head. I couldn't understand what was happening.

I looked for William to see if he knew what was going on, William told the doctor to explain to me what was wrong. The doctor said that Heather had a massive tumour behind her liver and it had just erupted. The cancer had spread through her entire body and there was nothing they could do. He told me that in his experience, if she made the next few hours then she might live for a few days.

It was unbelievable, just hours earlier I was laying my sister to rest, now I was being told my other sister could be dead within the next few hours or days. Sitting with me was my brother-in-law who had a brain tumour and was just told his wife was about to die. Our lives were just thrown into utter chaos, it just felt surreal. Shortly after this conversation, Heather fell asleep and she never woke again. She passed away peacefully. She died not knowing that her sister was already dead. Within the space of a week I had lost both of my sisters. It was a devastating time for us all.

Chapter Twenty-one
Grieving...

It was a very dark time. The grief was so difficult as I didn't know how to grieve for two sisters. Who do you grieve for first? I found myself thinking about one then trying to concentrate on the other. It was really difficult as they both went at the same time. Then I was trying to support my dad, their deaths really took their toll on him. My head was in a spin, I just didn't know how to compute what had just happened to our family.

The next Sunday, I was back on the pulpit, I felt like I had to keep going, otherwise it would have crippled me. I knew I was still in shock but I didn't want time to dwell on it. However, because I was back preaching then people thought that it was all over, so they started coming to me again with their problems and I just wasn't ready to deal with them.

In the next few weeks our church had a couple of deaths. It was during this time I realised there was such a thing as delayed shock and it was about to wrap itself around me.

Being at the funerals, seeing the grief just brought it all home to me. I started to break down and more so, feelings would surface with inner pain that was indescribable.

I also had a problem, I found out, a problem I had not shared with anyone. I was seeing God move mightily in healings, and yet my family had died. First my mum and now my two sisters. After a lot of wrestling with the Lord, I had to come to the conclusion that His Sovereignty supersedes my expectations, whether that's for the good or the bad times. I have to leave it to His Sovereign will, I can't work it out.

Not long after, my dad started to take ill. One day when we were visiting, Alison noticed an antibiotic sitting and had questioned him about it. He thought it was a bladder infection. Just a few days later, he was in with the doctor and he was told to go straight to the hospital. He rang me and I collected him and drove him there.

The hospital told me that he had a cancerous lump and they would operate to remove it. The doctors didn't seem to be too worried about it so we tried not to make a fuss.

He went through his operation and it seemed to go well, the doctor warned me that he would be in Intensive Care for a few days. However, the reality was, he was there for eleven days following the surgery. He then was moved to a ward, where he stayed for the whole month of December. I drove down to the hospital with Jodie on Christmas Eve and we were allowed to bring him home for Christmas. We were delighted that he was able to come and stay with us. The girls were really excited. Jodie gave her bedroom to her Grandad and we had Christmas together.

He was very frail so we had nurses coming and working with him every day. He stayed with us into the New Year, he just rested and was starting to get stronger. On New Year's Eve, we all sat around the bed with him, it was a special time together. He was recovering but he was very sleepy, I noticed he would just drift in and out at times when you were speaking to him.

One Wednesday I was down at the church talking to an architect, the church had grown so much now we were making plans to extend. We had purchased the adjacent land and I was talking through some ideas. Afterwards he came up to the house and as soon as I saw my dad I knew something wasn't right.

I rang the doctor, he arrived and rang for an ambulance. I went in the ambulance with him. They took him to the Royal, then transferred him to the City hospital. They performed tests and a couple of days later I got the call to come down.

Alison and I arrived and we were taken into a small room with the consultant, surgeon and nurse. They told us that the cancer was so aggressive that it was unstoppable. There was nothing they could do for him. It was devastating. I thought he was recovering but really, he was dying.

ALISON: I will never forget that room we were sitting in, the news came so hard. They told us first, then they were going to tell Ken's daddy.

Ken asked them how long was left and the consultant said it would probably be between four and six weeks. It was such hard news to take in.

I was really worried about how Ken was going to deal with this. We left the room and went to see his dad. I was very emotional, he looked so tiny lying there in the hospital bed. I just couldn't believe that he was dying.

Ken tried to explain to him what we had just been told and he was so brave taking it all in. It was like he already knew what was coming. Ken pulled up a chair beside him and took his hand, as he started to talk to him, he just broke. It was so hard. His dad said to him; "Come on now son, it's alright." He was the one who was dying but he was trying to comfort both of us, we were just so broken.

He was in the hospital for another few days then they took him to a hospice and he died ten days later with both his sons at his side.

Low times...

Things were so bad, I was feeling really low. It was a really hard, dark time. One day I took our Harley Davidson out. Harley is our dog! We had gone for a walk along the river bank and I was praying, he was swimming. As I watched him swim, every emotion was going through me, hurt, mourning, frustration, confusion. All these things were going on in my mind. When my dad died I remember just thinking that I wanted to be with him. Obviously, I wanted him to be with me but I thought if he can't then I wanted to go to him. At that point, life just felt like nothing, everything had been taken away from me. I really missed him, even to this day I still feel the loss of my father. I honestly thought at the time that it was going to be the death of me.

I thought back to a sermon I had delivered the Sunday morning that Heather was taken into the hospital. That Sunday morning I felt really strongly to change my sermon so I prayed and I changed my Scripture to Psalm 61:2; *'When my heart is overwhelmed: lead me to the rock that is higher than I.'*

I just opened with this Scripture and allowed the Lord to direct me from there, as I preached He put the words into my mouth. The idea of *'when my heart is overwhelmed'* is, when the centre of everything that I am, all that I am within me is covered or shrouded as though with a dark cloak. You can't see, you have nowhere to turn to, nowhere to go when such a calamity has hit you. Then your cry is, "Lead me to the rock that is higher."

As the rock is higher, then we can look down upon everything when we are on that high rock. It is there that we are above our problems, above our stresses, worries and fears. I preached on that theme that Christ is our rock. Little did I know that the Scripture wasn't for the church that morning, it was for me. Within hours of sharing that message, I was thrown into turmoil with my family.

I didn't know what was coming but the Lord knew and I believe He was preparing me. It's then taking the word of the Lord and letting it take root in your heart and your mind for when the circumstances come. It's having that word abide in you and seeing it, rather than what is going on around you. As Isaiah quotes in 43:2: '*When thou passest through the waters, I will be with thee; and through the rivers, they shall not overflow thee: when thou walkest through the fire, thou shalt not be burned; neither shall the flame kindle upon thee.*'

Through this time, the Lord kept giving me Scripture, even when I was by the river this Scripture would come to me. My past sermons would come flooding into my mind and I took my strength from that. Through this heartache the Lord was teaching me not to sympathise but to emphasise with people. When people in the church were experiencing loss, I was able to come alongside them and tell them how they would feel and think.

I continued preaching and the Lord worked in me and through me. It was a hard path to walk and at times I don't know if I would have got through it so well without Alison.

Further heartbreak...

We were just starting to catch our breath, slowly venturing back up the mountain again. I was encouraging Ken to grieve for his family when we suffered further heartbreak with William. This again, hit Ken hard as they had grown up together, they were friends before he became his brother-in-law.

We were going to visit William one day who had been a member of the RUC, (Northern Ireland Police) and decided to ring Alanah, his daughter before we left. We knew something was wrong as Alanah said that he was still sleeping, she had tried to waken him but he wasn't responding. She had just rang the doctor so we said we would leave straight away.

When we arrived at the house, the doctor was still there working with him. He still hadn't wakened and was in bad shape. Shortly after the doctor left, William was groaning then he took a massive seizure. Ken left the room to get help which left me on my own with William. It was an awful experience. I didn't know what to do, so I started to pray. I prayed aloud for God's help, Bradley, his son came in and must have thought I had lost it but at that time, I just didn't know what else to do. I felt a strong sense of peace come over me and then this clarity came. Bradley helped me to move William to make him more comfortable and to get his airways cleared.

A nurse then arrived to help us. She looked at him and told us not to move him any further, I explained we had only rolled him slightly in case he choked on his vomit. She told me that if we moved him, he would die. I just couldn't believe what I was hearing.

We knew William didn't want to die at home, he thought it would be too much for the children. He had made arrangements to go into a hospice but when Ken rang, it was full.

William's brothers then arrived and they were asking Ken what to do. They were all gathered around him looking for some guidance. Ken told them that William didn't want to die at home, so if the hospice couldn't take him, then they should let him go to the hospital. At least it was still following his wishes, so they all nodded in agreement, the decision was made.

The paramedics arrived and they took him to the hospital. He did make it to the Royal hospital but he died within hours of the journey. This left Alanah and Bradley to plan a funeral so they looked to Ken for help. The family was distraught. Thankfully the RUC really stepped in and helped with the funeral arrangements as William was highly respected in his job. They piped him in and it was a lovely funeral, just the respectful send-off that he deserved.

Chapter Twenty-two

A journey we did not expect...

It was now almost eight and a half years from I had taken the position of pastor in Donaghcloney Elim. Since being there, the congregation had grown from 14 to a full house, and more importantly while growing in numbers, they grew in their walk with Christ. In a short period of time 130 people went through the waters of baptism, in obedience to the Lord.

In May 2016 was the upcoming referendum for Brexit. Different members of the congregation had asked me to preach on it, they wanted to know what God's Word said about it. That night as I taught from the Scriptures and what I believed the Bible said, the packed church listened attentively as I preached on the European Union and as Christian's, how I felt we should be voting in regard to Brexit.

The service was recorded and posted on *YouTube* and in no time at all, it had over 3,500 views. People were really interested in this topic. Within the next week, we had over 1,000 copies of the DVD requested. In-fact the congregation was enlightened so much on the Brexit matter, they asked me to go deeper into what I had taught, they wanted a second part. I was hesitant about doing it but the people were really interested. Some churches met in their own buildings and watched the sermon via DVD. So, when they heard I was going deeper, the church was packed again for the second teaching on it. Churches across the United Kingdom from Scotland to London, from London to Londonderry, ordered copies to show in their meetings and house groups.

I shared the teaching openly and honestly on what I believed, holding to the truths of many pioneers of God's work and Pentecostal worthies such as the revered, respected and honoured, evangelist, Principle George Jeffries, one of the founders of the Elim movement. However, it later transpired that the Elim headquarters had heard about it and although they agreed with most of it, they didn't agree with all of it. I was then invited on 23rd June 2016 to the headquarters to discuss doctrinal differences.

They told me that some complaints had been received about my Brexit sermon and after discussing it at length, I was asked if there was any way I would change my mind about it before I went out the doors. I told them that I couldn't. How could I preach one thing then say the opposite? Would that not make me a hypocrite? They then said that I was incompatible with them and I said the same back to them.

Because I couldn't agree to what they requested they said they would have to take it to the ILT (Irish Leadership Team) to discuss it. They told me that they would come back to me shortly, they assured me that they wouldn't keep me hanging on.

When I saw Alison afterwards, I said to her; "I'm away. That's me out."

Two months later, there was still no word about the meeting. I had been asked to preach at a conference in America and as it was also my 50th birthday, Alison and the girls decided to come too and afterwards we would have a holiday while we were there. Alison was anxious about what was going to happen with the Elim church as we still hadn't heard anything. To ease her mind, I tried to chase the outcome but no-one was answering, so I left a few messages for them to contact me.

That Tuesday night, we were due to go America in the early hours but I went to the Bible study first while the girls packed up their clothes. I had just arrived at the church when my phone rang. An Elim official said; "Ken, I didn't want to talk to you over the phone about this."

I said; "Well, we are wondering what is going on?"

They said; "Yes, well we are going to ask you to leave."

"Oh right, I see."

"Will you come over and talk to us about it?"

"Well I am going to America in a few hours." I replied.

"Sorry to tell you that before you go to America."

I said; "That's okay, I will sort it out when I come back."

Your love must outweigh the pain...

I remember that night so clear as if it was only yesterday. The congregation all filed in for the Bible study, those who always came early, were still early, and the rest followed promptly behind. All eager to learn from the Word of God. Looking at their faces, I knew that God had put such a love in me for the Donaghcloney congregation, a love that no matter how much I felt pain, my love for them had to outweigh it. I had to carry on and hold the Bible study. Nobody knew what was going on in the church. I tried to act as normally as possible, concentrating on the congregation.

Afterwards I went home and told Alison what had happened, she was disappointed in the way I had been treated but she was also relieved as now at least we knew what was ahead of us when we would come back from America.

What a great blessing our trip and conference was as we found relief from the stresses at home and had great fellowship with some dear friends, Pastor Charles Jennings and his wife Marylee. The Christian love and support from them, and their congregation was immense and we had a real time of much-needed encouragement. God had them in the right place at the right time to show us His path in this dark season. To crown it all off, I was given the honour of being ordained into their ministry.

When we arrived back from the States, I started preparing others to take over from my duties. The people had no idea what was going on and I wondered how we would break the news to them.

An official meeting was arranged again to discuss the mechanics of my dismissal. Many questions were asked but it saddened me when they asked me if I was going to split the church. I of course told them that I wasn't. I would never do anything to jeopardise the church after spending so long building it up. I had put my heart and soul into seeing this grow. I told them that I would announce my leaving to the church but would ask the congregation all to stay.

I made the announcement in the church the following Sunday, I asked them all to be in attendance next Sunday as a very important announcement was going to be made concerning the church. That following Sunday morning I carried on with the service as per normal and at the end we had the breaking of bread. Afterwards I told the people that I had something to read to them and ensued to read a letter from the Elim HQ in Ireland, and another from myself. Both letters were polite and cordial but formal. Throughout all our discussions we never once had an argument nor even a raised voice in anger between us.

When I finished, people were crying in the congregation, it was awful. Everyone was in shock. They all got up silently and left the church, shell-shocked. By that evening however, it was a different matter, the church was in uproar. Obviously, they now had the time to digest the information given earlier and had talked to each other and they were not happy. They asked for a meeting with Elim HQ as they wanted me to stay.

Never had I heard of anyone being put out of the Elim for preaching a secondary doctrine so it was extremely controversial this happening, especially for our own congregation. Some people in the church had questioned me as to why I wouldn't just backtrack from what I had preached. I told them that I wanted to keep my integrity intact. I preached that sermon because it was what I believed, I wouldn't teach the people something then backtrack from it just to keep my job. I didn't think that would be right. Once they knew there was no way of me staying, many of them left the church.

The Elim leadership and I may have differed in the minor but in the major, we are one. I thank God for them for we are all workers in the great harvest field of this world.

I thought what would I do now? I decided to take a month off just to spend time with my family and concentrate on writing 'Finding God's Path in a Dark Season.' Little did I know when I started to write this book months earlier, another dark season regarding this chapter was about to enter. But praise the Lord, the greater Light, Jesus Christ outweighs any dark season. We must keep going, for the Light is always there whether we see it at the time or not!

Section 9

Following a new path

'And Jabez called on the God of Israel, saying, Oh that thou wouldest bless me indeed, and enlarge my coast, and that thine hand might be with me, and that thou wouldest keep me from evil, that it may not grieve me! And God granted him that which he requested.'

1 Chronicles 4:10

Chapter Twenty-three
Christ Encounters

For the next few months I was invited to preach all around the province in churches, mission halls and tent campaigns. Many people came to Jesus being saved and many healed, I started to feel a new freshness flowing through me.

I was happy and content, studying through the day and most nights out ministering somewhere, so establishing another church was not something that crossed my mind.

One day, out of the blue, I received a phone call from a lady who had been talking to a local counsellor, about an empty hall in Gilford, she asked me if I would be interested in it for a church premises and without thinking, I said no.

Shortly after that, a man approached me and asked if I would be interested in setting up a church in Gilford in an empty hall he knew of and I said... no again.

When a third person came along and asked me the same question, I started to wonder was this the Lord trying to tell me something?

I had been offered a position to minister full-time near Belfast and I thought that was the direction we were moving in but then the more I thought of it, the more I wondered, was this Ken Davidson working out his life or was God seeking to work out Ken's life?

I gave in and decided to visit the hall that these people were all referring me to in Gilford.

Here I was standing outside an old British Legion hall on Gilford's main street, nothing would ever make you naturally desire it for anything, and surely not a church.

On entering it, empty beer bottles were littered all around it, there were cigarette burns on the furniture and a few dilapidated chairs laying here and there. It had been empty for over two years and the smell of nicotine and alcohol could have choked a person, with the extremely large cobwebs everywhere, it was in dire condition or as we would say, *a right mess.*

I thought, maybe if it was cleared out, it would be a great place to have a few meetings, that was as far as I could see.

But what I could not see, was that God had laid it on the people's hearts to get behind a move He was about to implement.

All sorts of trades and skills were waiting their turn to enter the hall, as mums, dads and dare I say, kids were all inside clearing it and washing walls and furniture all down.

As Philippians 2:2 states; *'Be likeminded, having the same love, being of one accord, of one mind,'* and then God moved with salvations and healings.

In what was supposed to be just for a few meetings - a church was birthed!

When a door closes in our life, it can be deemed as a dark season, but I have learned over the years in walking with God, when darkness surrounds, a new day is about to dawn.

On May 5th 2017, *Christ Encounters Tabernacle* was born and we're on a new journey of freedom in our God. Many have asked about the name of our church. The answer is quite simple, when God is in our house (church) there will always be a Christ Encounter.

Jesus never came for us to attend a building that we call church but we are the Church. He came to reveal His Father in heaven so we would have a relationship with Him.

Six months on from writing this book, we can see God reveal His hand on this work and all we can say is; "This is the Lord's doing; it is marvellous in our eyes." For we are confident, *'That He* (Jesus) *who has begun a good work in you* (us) *will complete it until the day of Jesus Christ.'* Philippians 1:6.

As a pastor now for many years, I want to take this time to encourage you.

You may have never realised the type of life we led previously to being a Christian and afterwards, but in truth; it is not about how bad or good we were or are. It's about *'while we were yet sinners, Jesus still died for us.'* Romans 5:8.

Have we failed? Yes. Do we need forgiveness today? Yes. As a Christian, each day we need to rely more on God than yesterday. I pray that *Finding God's Path in a Dark Season* has brought light on your dark season and now please allow me to pray with you...

Almighty God,

I come to you in the name of your only begotten Son, the Lord Jesus Christ.

I realise that I cannot save myself and that He is the only Saviour.

I believe he died for me and he alone could pay my debt of sin in full, and I believe he did this once and for all when he shed his blood and gave up his life on Cavalry's cross.

I place my whole life into your hands and in your great grace and mercy I ask you to forgive me of all my sin and cleanse me from all unrighteousness as I come in repentance to you, turning away from my old life and turning to trust Jesus only, pleading the power of his shed blood.

Fill me with your Holy Spirit and lead me every day, give me the strength and the grace to confess you to my family and friends as Lord and Saviour over my life. I believe right now I am saved, I am a child of God. In the mighty name of Jesus.

Amen.

If you have prayed that prayer we would love to hear from you. If you are ever near Christ Encounters Tabernacle, we would love you to call in.

If we can help you in any way, feel free to contact us.

To contact Pastor Ken and Alison Davidson or to invite them to minister…

Email your enquiry to info@ChristEncounters.org

For further details visit www.ChristEncounters.org

A Glossary of Bible Verses for every Season...

Anxiety - *'Be careful for nothing; but in every thing by prayer and supplication with thanksgiving let your requests be made known unto God. And the peace of God, which passeth all understanding, shall keep your hearts and minds through Christ Jesus.'*
Philippians 4: 6-7.

Broken Heart - *'The Lord is nigh unto them that are of a broken heart; and saveth such as be of a contrite spirit.'*
Psalm 34:18.

Despair - *'Why art thou cast down, O my soul? and why art thou disquieted within me? hope in God: for I shall yet praise him, who is the health of my countenance, and my God.'*
Psalm 43:5.

Disappointment - *'And we know that all things work together for good to them that love God, to them who are the called according to his purpose.'*
Romans 8:28.

Doubt - *'And Jesus said unto them, Because of your unbelief: for verily I say unto you, If ye have faith as a grain of mustard seed, ye shall say unto this mountain, Remove hence to yonder place; and it shall remove; and nothing shall be impossible unto you.'*
Matthew 17:20.

Impatience - *'Wait on the Lord: be of good courage, and he shall strengthen thine heart: wait, I say, on the Lord.'*
Psalm 27:14.

Impossibilities - *'And he said, The things which are impossible with men are possible with God.'*
Luke 18:27.

Lacking Direction - *'Trust in the Lord with all thine heart; and lean not unto thine own understanding. In all thy ways acknowledge him, and he shall direct thy paths.'*
Proverbs 3: 5-6.

Lacking Wisdom - *'But of him are ye in Christ Jesus, who of God is made unto us wisdom, and righteousness, and sanctification, and redemption.'*
I Corinthians 1:30.

Loneliness - *'Be strong and of a good courage, fear not, nor be afraid of them: for the Lord thy God, he it is that doth go with thee; he will not fail thee, nor forsake thee.'*
Deuteronomy 31:6.

Mourning - *'Blessed are they that mourn: for they shall be comforted.'*
Matthew 5:4.

Poverty - *'But my God shall supply all your need according to his riches in glory by Christ Jesus.'*
Philippians 4:19.

Sickness - *'My son, attend to my words; incline thine ear unto my sayings. Let them not depart from thine eyes; keep them in the midst of thine heart. For they are life unto those that find them, and health to all their flesh.'*
Proverbs 4:20-22.

Sorrow - *'Then shall the virgin rejoice in the dance, both young men and old together: for I will turn their mourning into joy, and will comfort them, and make them rejoice from their sorrow.'*
Jeremiah 31:13.

Temptation - *'There hath no temptation taken you but such as is common to man: but God is faithful, who will not suffer you to be tempted above that ye are able; but will with the temptation also make a way to escape, that ye may be able to bear it.'*
1 Corinthians 10:13.

Tiredness - *'But they that wait upon the Lord shall renew their strength; they shall mount up with wings as eagles; they shall run, and not be weary; and they shall walk, and not faint.'*
Isaiah 40:31.

Weariness - *'Come unto me, all ye that labour and are heavy laden, and I will give you rest. Take my yoke upon you, and learn of me; for I am meek and lowly in heart; and ye shall find rest unto your souls. For my yoke is easy, and my burden is light.'*
Matthew 11:28-30.

Weariness - *'I can do all things through Christ which strengtheneth me.'*
Philippians 4:13.

Worry - *'Casting all your care upon him; for he careth for you.'*
1 Peter 5:7.

INSPIRED TO WRITE A BOOK?

Contact
Maurice Wylie Media
Inspirational Christian Publisher

Based in Northern Ireland and distributing across the world
www.MauriceWylieMedia.com